VAT: A PR
HA

TEACH YOURSELF BOOKS

VAT: A PRACTICAL HANDBOOK

David Lee
VAT Control Officer, Customs and Excise

TEACH YOURSELF BOOKS
Hodder and Stoughton

British Library Cataloguing in Publication Data
Lee, David
VAT: a practical handbook.
I. Title
336.200941

ISBN 0-340-55843-1

First published 1991

Typeset by Rowland Phototypesetting Ltd, Bury St Edmunds, Suffolk
Printed in Great Britain for the educational publishing division of Hodder & Stoughton Ltd, Mill Road, Dunton Green, Sevenoaks, Kent by Clays Ltd, St Ives plc.

Acknowledgements

The author and publishers would like to thank the Controller of Her Majesty's Stationery Office for permission to reproduce and adapt Customs and Excise leaflets.

Contents

Preface

VAT was introduced as a simple tax.
Income Tax was introduced as a temporary measure.
The *Titanic* was introduced as an unsinkable ship.

Value Added Tax is an inescapable part of European Community life. Businesses charge it, consumers pay it. If you are in business, whether in England, Wales, Scotland or Northern Ireland, your business activities are subject to the one United Kingdom VAT law.

Official literature on United Kingdom VAT and regulations runs to well over 100 publications. Some of these can easily be understood, others require time and a box of headache pills before giving up their secrets. Yet ignorance is never accepted as an excuse if you make a mistake. There are no prizes for getting your VAT right, but financial restitution together with penalties, surcharges and interest is demanded from those who get it wrong.

This book is a guide to United Kingdom VAT, its complexities and its oddities. Fortunately a large part of VAT is fairly straightforward. Unfortunately the rest ranges from the complex to the illogical. The following pages are designed, in plain English, to give you a good grasp of the subject as well as setting you on the right tracks for a fair weather passage through your VAT registered life.

David Lee

1

Introduction to VAT

What exactly is Value Added Tax? · Registration · Your Tax Periods · Your Tax Return · Interest and Penalty

What exactly is Value Added Tax?

VAT is simply a tax on customer spending. It is *not* a tax on the business which charges it, but on whoever buys from it. Put another way, VAT is a tax which consists of value being added to a sale by a business which then sends this value via a VAT return to Customs and Excise, who collect and administer the tax on behalf of the government. This sale can be either a sale of goods or a sale of services.

If you are in business you have to register with Customs and Excise, and charge VAT, if what is called your 'taxable turnover' goes over certain monetary limits within a 12-month time span. Your taxable turnover is simply the amount or value of all your sales or transactions (the technical word for these is 'supplies') that carry or are liable to VAT.

Once you are registered for VAT you have to start completing a **VAT return**, usually once every three months. This is simply a case of adding up all the VAT you have charged – your **output tax** – and subtracting from it the total VAT your business has itself been charged – your **input tax**. If the difference is in Customs and Excise's favour then you pay them that difference. If, however, the difference is in your favour then Customs and Excise will pay you that difference.

Unfortunately, VAT has many complications and has become something of a minefield. But if you can grasp the basics, understand the jargon that is used, and know where to look for help, you are well on the way to avoiding the traps which most people fall into. Do try and memorise the jargon because you will find it coming up all the time in your dealings with Customs and Excise. You will find a glossary at the end of the book for easy reference.

Customs and Excise

Note that it is Customs and Excise who look after VAT. If you have not yet done so, it would be a very good idea to look up your **local VAT office** (LVO for short) in the telephone directory under 'Customs and Excise' and make a note of the number. This is because every LVO has an enquiries office whose job it is to answer your questions. You might also see an entry for a VAT sub office (or VSO) but these have no enquiries function.

Apart from answering queries your LVO will have a stock of VAT notices and VAT leaflets. If you do not yet have any of these publications, why not ring up and ask for the following ones? They are all directly relevant to this first chapter and cover the basic elements of VAT:

- Notice 700 'The VAT Guide'. This is the general publication on VAT but it is very heavy going, best kept for reference.
- VAT Leaflet 700/13 or 13A 'VAT publications'. This one is handy because on the order form at the back you can request any publication you might find useful. The leaflet itself is merely a list of all VAT publications.
- VAT Leaflet 701/39 'VAT liability law'. This is a list stating what is zero-rated and what is exempt – more on this in a moment.
- 700/1 'Should I be registered for VAT?'
- 700/12 'Filling in your VAT return'.
- 700/42 'Serious misdeclaration penalty'. More on this and 700/43 'Default interest' at the end of this chapter.

Customs and Excise and the Inland Revenue

When thinking about VAT it is important to remember that Customs and Excise and the Inland Revenue are quite separate civil service departments. As a rule, the Inland Revenue deals with direct taxation, that is taxes on your income, whereas Customs and

Excise deal with indirect taxation, that is taxes which *you* collect and pass on to *them*.

It is also worth noting that when you deal with the Inland Revenue, your affairs are under the scrutiny of a tax inspector, but with Customs and Excise you will deal with an officer of Customs and Excise, just like the officers who patrol the 'goods to declare' channels at ports and airports.

You are, in fact, an unpaid tax collector when you are VAT registered. Not only that, but it is *your* responsibility to make sure that *you* get it right. To encourage you to do this there are financial penalties for those who get it wrong. There is more on this at the end of the chapter, but the golden rule to keep in mind throughout your VAT registered life is that all Customs and Excise want from you is *the right tax at the right time*.

Supplies – Standard-rated, Zero-rated or Exempt

A supply is a transaction, a sale or provision of services. The **liability** of a supply is whether it should be taxed (and at which rate) or not. Thus a **taxable supply** is one which is liable to tax at either the standard or the zero rate.

The standard rate

This is currently at 17.5%. The majority of supplies are **standard-rated**, but the law avoids having to list them all by saying that everything not specifically **zero-rated** or **exempt** from VAT is standard-rated. This is a very important point, because it means that if you are VAT registered you should *always* charge VAT unless you are certain you are entitled not to do so.

The zero rate

Although it is zero this is still a rate of tax, because all that has happened is that the rate has been set at nil. As mentioned above, do make sure that something qualifies for zero-rating before you charge no VAT. Examples of zero-rated supplies include food (although catering is standard-rated), books and children's clothing. Remember, a zero-rated supply is still a taxable supply and is not to be confused with exempt supplies.

Exempt supplies

This means that the supply is exempt from VAT. No VAT can be charged – it is not a taxable supply. If you make only exempt supplies you cannot register for VAT because you cannot charge it.

Examples of exempt supplies include certain supplies of land and property, insurance, finance, burial services and education (see Chapter 4). The list is a fairly specialised one, but what might well happen is that you find yourself making both taxable and exempt supplies. For example, you may own a shop selling taxable items, but you might also own the flat above and rent it out. The problem comes when you want to reclaim input tax which relates to that exempt supply (for example on repairs to the flat). This is where things become quite complicated because you might not be able to claim all the input tax back – Chapter 4 on **partial exemption** goes into this in some depth.

Outside the Scope

This is the term given to supplies which are neither standard-rated, zero-rated nor exempt. Supplies made outside the United Kingdom are outside the scope of UK VAT. Curiously, the Isle of Man is part of the UK as far as VAT goes but the Channel Islands are not.

A supply is also outside the scope if it is not made as a business supply. For example, you might have a hobby collecting teddy bears, occasionally selling one or two. This would be classed as outside the scope. But if your hobby increased to a point where you were starting to buy and sell lots of teddy bears it might then be considered a business. If that happened you would be well advised to contact your local VAT office for advice on whether or not you should register.

If you are employed by a firm and paid a wage or salary from which Income Tax is deducted, this too is outside the scope of VAT. But if you are self-employed and work for the same firm then your supply is within the scope of VAT and might well be taxable.

Supplies – Goods and Services

Supplies are either goods or services. What this means is that if you are not supplying goods you are supplying services. Interestingly, a supply of heat, refrigeration, ventilation or power is a supply of goods whereas hiring equipment out which heats, refrigerates, ventilates or powers is a supply of services.

Even more interestingly, *not* doing something in return for some form of payment is a supply of services. Taking goods out of your business for yourself counts as a supply of goods but lending them to someone to use outside your business is a supply of services. Here is an example of how this difference might well affect you: suppose your business buys a car. Now a car is one of the few business expenses on which you cannot reclaim the VAT when you purchase it. Obviously here a car is a supply of goods to you. If, however, your business leases or hires the car, you can claim back the VAT because this is now a supply of services to you as you do not get to keep the car. But, if buried in the small print of the contract there is a clause giving you an option to purchase, so that in effect the car is being bought on lease-purchase or hire-purchase, the supply reverts to being one of goods on which you would not be entitled to reclaim VAT.

Supplies Not Made for Money

Sometimes you may not deal in hard cash. For example, you may trade in an old piece of machinery for a new one or you may be paid partly in special offer coupons. This is why Customs and Excise talk in terms of a **consideration** for a supply, or, more simply, whatever you receive in return for supplying something. When this happens, VAT is due on the full value. Put another way, you have to pay the same amount of VAT as if you had received the whole price in money.

Working Out the VAT – The VAT Fraction

VAT is charged at 17.5%. To work out the VAT on something you are selling, you decide on your selling price and *add* 17.5% to it. So goods you want to sell for £100 will be sold for £100 + 17.5% (which is £17.50) = £117.50.

Note that £17.50 is 17.5% of £100 – it is *not* 17.5% of the final selling price of £117.50. To get the VAT element from the final selling price you multiply by the **VAT fraction**:

$$\frac{\text{rate of tax}}{100 + \text{rate of tax}}$$

The current rate of VAT is 17.5%, so when this is put into the calculation it is:

$$\frac{17.5}{100 + 17.5} = \frac{17.5}{117.5} = \frac{7}{47}$$

So to go back to the example above, to find the VAT element of the final selling price of £117.50, simply multiply by 7 and divide by 47:

$$£117.50 \times \frac{7}{47} = £17.50$$

Registration

This is the first hurdle you have to clear, right at the start of your VAT registered life. If you register at the wrong time you may be hit with a financial penalty, so do take the time to make sure you understand the who, how and why of registration.

Taxable Turnover

Remember, you have to register with Customs and Excise if the taxable turnover of your business goes over certain limits, i.e. the registration limit. Note that it is the value of your turnover and *not* the value of your profit which determines whether or not you have to register. Note also that you have to be in business to register – you cannot register if you merely want to reclaim VAT on a hobby.

Here is an example of the type of decision you will have made before registering. You decide you want to become an airline pilot, but the only way you can do this is to pay for the training yourself. So you decide to register to try to reclaim the VAT on training costs. Now if it is your intention to be employed by an airline your registration will be refused because you will not be making taxable supplies. But if it is your intention to run your own airline you will be making taxable supplies and so you will be registered.

Remember, too, that taxable supplies are both standard *and* zero-rated supplies but *not* exempt supplies. Make sure you know which, if any, of your supplies are exempt because these do not count when you register (see Chapter 4 for a list of exempt supplies).

Apart from taxable supplies you have made, you should also include in the value of your taxable turnover any money you have received in advance for taxable supplies you will make under a contract. Interestingly, services you receive from abroad such as consultancy services or hire of goods are also included in your taxable turnover (see Chapter 6 for a full list). This is to prevent unfair competition with UK suppliers.

Who and What Your Registration Covers

Although the word 'business' has been used until now, it is not in fact the business that is registered, it is the *person*. In VAT terms a **'VAT registered person'** means the entity which is in business. Your VAT registration covers all the business activities of your particular 'entity'. Your entity or status can be one of the following:

Sole proprietor
This is for the sole trader. But remember that your registration will cover all your business activities, so if you run, say, a camera shop in the week and a circus at the weekend, your registration will cover both activities.

Partnership
This is for anyone who runs a business together with another person or persons (including your husband or your wife).

Limited company
This is for both the company with a 'Ltd' after its name and for the company with 'plc' after its name. Setting up a limited company is obviously a matter for discussion between you and your accountant, as there are certain advantages and disadvantages in doing so. On the plus side there are tax and insolvency advantages. On the minus side there may be problems raising finance.

Sometimes a group of limited companies may wish to combine as one VAT registration, and this can be done as a group registration. On the other hand one limited company may wish to register by section, and this can be done as a divisional registration.

A charity, club or association
If you are involved in setting up any of these, they can register in their own right.

Remember, your VAT registration covers your particular 'person'. So if you are registered as a sole proprietor to run your camera shop and circus but then start up a road haulage firm at nights as a partnership, you will be creating another entity and you will have to register that separately. Technically this is called a **Change of Legal Entity**.

When to Register

Now for the important part. It is absolutely vital that you register at the right time because you have to start charging and accounting for any VAT from the date the law requires you to register. If later you are found to have registered too late your registration will be back-dated to the correct date. If this happens you will have to account for any VAT due from the earlier date to when you actually registered. You will also be charged a penalty, but more on this in a moment.

Having identified your taxable turnover, the next step is to put a value on it. You should be aware of how much you are taking, day by day, week by week, so it should simply be a case of watching for when you approach the registration limit.

The Registration Limit

At the end of each month work out the value of your taxable turnover for the last 12 months (or from the time you started if it is less) up to the month end you are at. If it is more than the registration limit (currently £35,000) then you have to be registered. The registration limit usually alters at each budget so do be aware of any change.

Telling the VAT Office

It is the end of the month. Your taxable turnover has gone over the limit. You now have 30 days to submit your **notification**, which means filling in Form **VAT 1** to tell your local VAT office that you have to be registered.

On the VAT 1 (there is a specimen copy at the end of this section with some notes to help you fill it in) you have to give your registration date. To find this date, you take the month end date when you found that you had to register, leave out the next month and your registration date is the first day of the following month.

This sounds complicated, but here is a table to help you work out exactly what you should do.

Date you found your taxable turnover exceeded the limit:	**Fill in form VAT 1 to notify VAT office by:**	**Registration date to go on your VAT 1**
31 January	2 March	1 March
28 (or 29) February	30 March	1 April
31 March	30 April	1 May
30 April	30 May	1 June
31 May	30 June	1 July
30 June	30 July	1 August
31 July	30 August	1 September
31 August	30 September	1 October
30 September	30 October	1 November
31 October	30 November	1 December
30 November	30 December	1 January
31 December	30 January	1 February

These dates apply if you have simply gone over the registration limit.

If, before you reach the registration limit, you have what are termed 'reasonable grounds' to believe that your taxable turnover will go over the registration limit in the next 30 days, you also have to register. You have to fill in Form VAT 1 and notify the VAT office within 30 days of when you first knew, or had a good idea that you would go over the limit.

An example of this situation is where you might sign a contract and you can see from what is involved that it will put you over the limit. The date of registration you have to put on Form VAT 1 is the date when these 'reasonable grounds' first existed, in this case the date you signed the contract.

Late Registration

If you get all this wrong and notify too late, not only does your registration get backdated, but you have to account for any VAT due on supplies you made from that date. You also get a penalty.

The penalty is calculated by looking at exactly how late you were in registering. You are charged a percentage of the net VAT due from the date you should have registered to the date you put on Form VAT 1 as being your date of registration. Up to 9 months late the penalty is 10%, up to 18 months late it is 20%, and over 18 months late the penalty is 30%.

However, you can escape the penalty if you have what is termed a 'reasonable excuse'. Each one is treated on its merits but it is worth noting that the law only defines what is *not* an excuse. These are:

- Having no money
- Relying on someone else who has got it wrong

So if your accountant fails to tell you to register you cannot escape the penalty by blaming him or her.

If this affects you, the leaflet to get hold of is 700/41 'Late registration – penalties and reasonable excuse'. Make no mistake, you need a good excuse like serious illness before you are in with a chance. Nevertheless, if you do have an excuse it may well be worth a try. (If you appeal and Customs and Excise reject your excuse the way is open for you to go to a **VAT Tribunal** – see Chapter 9.) However, obviously the ideal situation is where you avoid the penalty by getting it right first time round.

Special Registrations

Transferring a Business

If you take over another business you can register your new business as a **'Transfer of a going concern'** (TOGC). You can even, if you want it, keep the old VAT registration number.

Inevitably there are complications in doing it this way rather than having the previous owner deregister and then registering yourself from scratch. You have to satisfy certain conditions and, very important, if you take on the old VAT number you have to take on any debts that go with it. The only time this would be worthwhile would be if you changed your legal entity – if you stopped being a sole proprietor and became a partnership or limited company, for example. At least then you would know exactly what the old registration had been up to.

The relevant leaflet is 700/9 'Transfer of a business as a going concern'.

Registration Before Your Business is Up and Running

You may want to register right from the very start, for example if you are having a factory built and want to reclaim the VAT on it before you actually begin to manufacture anything. A beneficial side effect of registering early will be that you will avoid the penalties for registering late. Getting yourself registered in a situation like this means writing a letter to Customs and Excise with your VAT 1 stating your circumstances. You should also send in any supporting evidence which will help your case (contracts, plans and planning permission, for example). You are setting yourself up as an **intending trader**.

If you do register and reclaim any VAT there should be no problem, but of course if you end up not making any taxable supplies you will have to pay any reclaimed VAT back again.

Voluntary Registration

This is for people who never make it to the registration limit but still want to be registered. Some firms do not like it if you are not registered and of course you will be able to reclaim the VAT on your business purchases and expenses. On the other side of the coin you have to face the same responsibilities and possible pitfalls as every other VAT registered person. Again you have to state your case when you send in your VAT 1, but you can choose your date of registration.

If You Do Not Want to be Registered

If you go over the registration limit and stay there you have to register and stay registered. But if your supplies are only zero-rated you can ask for exemption from registration. You still have to fill in Form VAT 1 and state your case, as you cannot assume you do not have to register. You can also apply for exemption if some of your supplies are standard-rated, and as long as Customs and Excise are happy you would pay less than you claim there should be no problem. On the plus side you would have no VAT paperwork or responsibilities. However, on the minus side you could not reclaim any VAT on your expenses, and if your circumstances change – for example, your standard-rated sales increase dramatically – you will have to register properly.

One other situation in which you may find you do not wish to register is when you reach the registration limit but immediately drop under it again and stay there. For example, if you run a bed and breakfast business you might have one exceptional season with no hope of another which sends you just over the limit. Again you have to fill in Form VAT 1 and ask for exemption.

Deregistration

This is much more simple as it only requires a letter. You must cancel your registration if you stop trading, stop making taxable supplies, sell, transfer your business or if you change your legal entity (in which case you may consider transferring it as a going concern). You can also ask to be deregistered if your turnover sinks below the registration limit. There are conditions for deregistering, for example you have to account for VAT on any stocks and assets (you will have reclaimed the VAT on these when you bought them) unless the VAT involved is less than £250. The relevant leaflet is 700/11 'Should I cancel my registration?'

Filling in Form VAT 1

This form (shown on p. 13) is fairly straightforward. Just remember one letter to one box and a gap of a box between words so that you do not confuse the computer.

Question 1
Before you write anything look at Question 4 as well. Ensure that the status you tick in Question 4 is the same as the status, or entity, you give in Question 1. So if you are a sole proprietor you put in

your full name. If you trade as a partnership you can put either the name of the partnership or the names of the partners (which might be tricky if there are more than one or two). Do not, however, confuse the name of your partnership or the names of your partners with Question 2, your trading name, if it happens to be different.

If you trade as a limited company simply enter the company's name with 'Ltd' or 'plc' after it. Note that the form requires the date of incorporation. You cannot, if you are a limited company, register before this date.

Question 4 also asks for your business activity and **trade class**. You will find your trade class number from Leaflet VAT 41 which is sent with the Form VAT 1. You simply choose the group that best describes your business (the number is for the benefit of the computer).

Question 2
If you have a trading name that is different to the name you put in Question 1, this is where you put it.

Question 3
Think for a moment before you fill in your address. You have to give the address that best fits the words **principal place of business**. For most businesses this should cause no difficulty, but if you are constantly moving around the country it could be a bit tricky. Remember, all correspondence will go to the address you enter here. If you move around frequently you might consider changing your principal place of business every time you move. It is absolutely vital you receive your VAT returns because if you do not fill them in on time you will run into problems (see Chapter 9).

Question 4
See Question 1.

Questions 5 and 6
If you tick box 5 remember to include details of your other registrations. If you tick box 6 do not forget to send details of your computer.

Questions 7 and 8
Tick box 7 if you are a **repayment trader**, i.e. your input tax each tax period exceeds your output tax so you usually get money back, for example, if you only make zero-rated supplies. Your bank details (Question 8) are then very important as you will be paid by credit transfer.

VALUE ADDED TAX

Application for Registration

HM Customs and Excise

For official use

Local office code and issuing number

Date of receipt 1

Local office code and registration number

Name

Trade name

Taxable turnover E D R D M Y Stagger Status

Rept. Vol. Oversize name address Computer user Group Div. Intg. Overseas

Bn D M Y

You should open up this form and read the notes before you answer these questions. Please write clearly in ink.

Applicant and business

1 Full name

2 Trading name

3 Address of principal place of business

Phone no.

Postcode

Business details

4 Status of business

Limited company Company incorporation certificate no. and date day month year 19

Sole proprietor Partnership Other–specify

Business activity Trade classification

5 Other VAT registrations

6 Do you use a computer for accounting?

7 Repayments of VAT

Bank account details

8 Bank sorting code and account no. National Girobank account no.

VAT 1

please continue overleaf →

Compulsory registrations

9 Are you required to be registered because the value of the taxable supplies:

	YES	NO
(a) you **have made** in the past 12 months or less has exceeded the registration limit?	☐	☐
OR		
(b) you **expect to make** in the next 30 days will exceed the registration limit?	☐	☐

10 • Date from which you:
(a) are required to be registered — day ☐ month ☐ year 19☐

(b) wish to be registered if earlier than (a) — day ☐ month ☐ year 19☐

• Value of expected taxable supplies in the 12 months from date of registration – (a) or (b) above — £

11 Exemption from compulsory registration ☐

expected value of zero-rated supplies in the next 12 months — £

Voluntary and intending registration

12 Taxable supplies below registration limits ☐

value of taxable supplies in the last 12 months — £

13 No taxable supplies made yet ☐

(a) expected annual value of taxable supplies — £

(b) expected date of first taxable supply — day ☐ month ☐ year 19☐

Business changes and transfers

14 Business transferred as a going concern ☐

(a) date of transfer or change of legal status — day ☐ month ☐ year 19☐

(b) name of previous owner

(c) previous VAT registration number (if known)

15 Transfer of VAT registration number
(You must also complete a form VAT 68) ☐

Declaration – You must complete this declaration

16 I ______________________________
(Full name in BLOCK LETTERS)

declare that all the entered details and information in any accompanying documents are correct and complete

Signature ______________________ Date ______________

Proprietor ☐ Partner ☐ Director ☐ Company Secretary ☐ Authorised Official ☐ Trustee ☐

For Official Use

Registration	Obligatory	Exemption	Voluntary	Intending	Transfer of Regn. no.
Approved – Initial/Date					
Refused – Initial/Date					
Form Issued – Initial/Date	VAT 9/ Other	VAT 8	VAT 7	Letter	Approval Letter

VAT1 F3733

Questions 9 to 15
These relate to the type of registration you either have to have, or are requesting. Questions 9 and 10 are for those of you who must register. Note that if you put a date in 10(b), which is for those who want an earlier date of registration, that date will be your registration date and you will have to account for any VAT due from that date. Note also that you still have to fill in Questions 9 and 10 if you fill in Question 11 when you request exemption from registration.

If you are filling in Questions 12 and 13 for voluntary registration and registration before your business is up and running, do not forget your covering letter and any evidence. If you are transferring a business and filling in Questions 14 and 15, remember that transferring the VAT number means transferring the debts. If you do tick box 15 you also have to fill in Form VAT 68.

Question 16
You can only sign here if you are one of the people next to one of the boxes underneath. Nobody else can sign it.

Your Tax Periods

Once you are registered you will receive a certificate of registration. Apart from showing your registration details it will give you the all-important dates of your **tax periods**. Every single day you are VAT registered falls into a tax period. A tax period is simply a length of time at the end of which you have to account for the VAT which belongs to that period. This you do by filling in your VAT return which covers that period (more on this in the next section). Normally your VAT return will cover three calendar months.

Have a look at the specimen VAT return in the next section. You will see the dates covered in the return in the top left-hand corner where it says, 'Value Added Tax Return for the period _______ to _______'. Over on the right you will also see a box with the word 'Period' above it – the period reference. So if the box has a period reference of 03 92 the return dates on the top left will run from 01 01 92 to 31 03 92. Do take care to make sure you know when your tax periods run from and up to because you will be penalised if you do not render the right tax at the right time (see the section on Interest and Penalty at the end of this chapter).

To spread out the influx of VAT returns over the year Customs and Excise will put you into one of three groups of tax periods:

Group 1	**Group 2**	**Group 3**
1 January to 31 March	1 February to 30 April	1 March to 31 May
1 April to 30 June	1 May to 31 July	1 June to 31 August
1 July to 30 September	1 August to 31 October	1 September to 30 November
1 October to 31 December	1 November to 31 January	1 December to 28/29 February

Changing Your Tax Periods

It may be that you are put into a group that is awkward for you. For example, your financial year may run to the end of January but your tax periods may run to the end of March, June, September and December. If this is the case simply write to your local VAT office saying which group of tax periods would suit you best. To get you into a new group of tax periods Customs and Excise will give you a return which is either longer or shorter than the normal 3 month return, so do pay attention to the precise length of time it will cover.

Tax periods normally cover calendar months. However, you might find working to calendar months awkward – for example, you may wish to tie in your tax periods to a financial year which finishes on an odd date such as 28 January, or you may wish your tax periods to end on the last Friday of the quarter for administrative reasons. If this is the case you can apply to your local VAT office (in writing) for your tax periods to fit in exactly with your requirements. You will be registered for **non-standard tax periods** and will then get a new certificate of registration showing your new details. Once again, do examine it carefully so you know exactly which dates your tax periods cover.

Repayment Traders

If you are in a position where you get money back with each return, for example if you only sell zero-rated goods, you can ask to be put onto monthly returns. On the plus side you will receive your money all the quicker, but remember you will have to fill in 12 VAT returns each year instead of the usual 4. Again it is a case of writing to your local VAT office to ask for this. If yours is a voluntary registration you cannot have monthly returns. Likewise, if your business changes so you transfer from being a repayment trader to paying money with every return, you will be put back onto quarterly returns.

Your Tax Return

For each and every tax period Customs and Excise will send you a VAT return to complete. This is Form **VAT 100** and a specimen is reproduced on page 18. When you read the following section on Interest and Penalty you will see that filling it in correctly is of the utmost importance.

The Form

The form will be printed with your name, address and VAT registration number as well as with the period details. Over on the right, under the registration number and period boxes, is a space where the 'due date' is entered. This is the day your return and any money due have to be sent in by. If you send them in late not only will Customs and Excise start sending you bills for what they think you owe, but they will also start surcharging you (see Chapter 9).

Do not alter any of the details that are printed on the form. If you change your address, for example, you should write instead to your local VAT office with the details. This is because your VAT return goes to the VAT Central Unit, VCU for short, which is purely a computer processing operation.

As you can see, it is a fairly simple form with a maximum of 8 boxes to fill in. Read the notes on the back before you write anything as they tell you exactly what to put in and leave out, especially when filling in boxes 4 and 5, the value of your **outputs** and your **inputs**.

Filling It In

Note that boxes 1–5 should always be filled in, even if for some reason you have nothing to write – for example, if you stop trading for any reason. If this is the case simply write 'none' in the boxes. If you do not do this Customs and Excise will assume that you are still trading and send you a bill, or central assessment, as if you had sent in the return late.

Note too that box 1, the VAT due, minus box 2, the VAT reclaimed, should always equal box 3, the amount you owe Customs and Excise or they owe you. If you are sending money do not forget to tick the box to the left of the declaration. More importantly, do not forget to send the money with the return because if it does not arrive before the 'due date' you will be in default and you may get a surcharge (see Chapter 9).

HM Customs and Excise

Value Added Tax Return

For the period

to

Registration number | Period

You could be liable to a financial penalty if your completed return and all the VAT payable are not received by the due date.

Due date:

For official use	

Fold here

Before you fill in this form please read the notes on the back. Complete all boxes clearly in ink, writing 'none' where necessary. Don't put a dash or leave any box blank. If there are no pence write "00" in the pence column. Do not enter more than one amount in any box.

		£	p
VAT due in this period on **sales** and other outputs	1		
VAT reclaimed in this period on **purchases** and other inputs	2		
Net VAT to be paid to Customs or reclaimed by you **(Difference between boxes 1 and 2)**	3		
Value of **outputs** (pounds only) excluding any VAT	4		00
Value of **inputs** (pounds only) excluding any VAT	5		00

Retail schemes. If you have used any of the schemes in the period covered by this return please enter the appropriate letter(s) in this box.

If you are enclosing a payment please tick (✓) this box.	DECLARATION by the signatory to be completed by or on behalf of the person named above. I, ...declare that the (Full name of signatory in BLOCK LETTERS) information given above is true and complete. Signature ....Date ....19..........

VAT 100 CD 1942/N1(8.89) F 3790(JANUARY 1990)

Finally, if you are a retailer (see Chapter 5) you have to show which **retail scheme** you have used to calculate your output tax. Then all that remains to be done is to sign and date the form, and to send it off with any money due in sufficient time to meet the deadline.

If you fill in your return incorrectly – for example, if the figures in box 1 minus those in box 2 do not equal those in box 3 – the VAT Central Unit will send it back to you for correction. Do make sure you then return it again by the date specified.

Deciding what to put in your VAT return is the subject of Chapter 2, but the following section shows why it is of the utmost importance that you get this right, on time, every time.

Interest and Penalty

As a VAT registered person your relationship with Customs and Excise will follow one of two paths. Either you will get it right or you will get it wrong. If you get it right you will generally be ignored. If, however, you get it wrong, Customs and Excise will encourage you onto the right tracks by means of various financial inducements which *you* will have to pay *them* to compensate for *your* errors.

Assuming that your VAT returns are submitted on time together with any money due (see Chapter 9 for what happens if they are not), your main concern should be to avoid making any mistakes that would mean being hit with interest and possibly a penalty too.

These are called, to give them their full names, **default interest** and **serious misdeclaration penalty**. The idea is to encourage you to submit VAT returns which are 100% accurate by punishing you financially if you do not. If you are planning to get someone else to compile your VAT return it is worth bearing in mind that you will still have to pay for that someone else's mistakes. After all, anyone can hit the wrong button on a calculator.

So, if you are visited by a VAT officer and he or she finds you have made a mistake, you are in for a bigger bill than the amount of the error. If you discover the error yourself the rules work slightly differently (see Chapter 9 on how to correct errors you yourself discover).

Default Interest

This is charged by Customs and Excise on any mistakes they discover to make up for the fact that you have had the use of the amount in question when it should have been in the government's coffers. So from the date this amount should have been paid to the date the VAT officer discovers the error and sends you a bill, or **assessment**, to recover it, you will have to pay interest at the going rate.

A small crumb of comfort is that it is a simple rate of interest rather than a compound one (so you will not be charged interest on interest if you delay paying the bill). The rate is actually set lower than the base rate, and this is because you cannot deduct it from your gross profit when working out what you owe to the Inland Revenue (as you can with interest on any commercial loans you take out).

Serious Misdeclaration Penalty

This is what you have to pay to Customs and Excise if the error you have made, and which is discovered by a visiting VAT officer, is considered to be sufficiently serious. All things being relative, the mistake is compared to the amount you should have paid, and, if it is equal to or more than 30% of this amount it is considered to be a 'serious misdeclaration'.

The penalty imposed is 20% of this misdeclared amount. This is obviously a very draconian punishment for ordinary mistakes, so do be aware of it and ensure that you avoid it.

Because larger firms paying £33333 or more on each VAT return are less likely to make mistakes amounting to 30% of what they should pay, the penalty also applies if the mistake is equal to, or greater than £10000 or 5% of the amount they should have paid.

Summary

- If you should have paid between £1 and £33333 on your VAT return the penalty applies if your error is 30% or more of the amount you should have paid.
- If you should have paid between £33333 and £200000 on your VAT return the penalty applies if your mistake is £10000 or more.
- If you should have paid £200000 or more on your VAT return the penalty applies if your error is 5% or more of the amount you should have paid.

Example

Suppose you fill in your VAT return and declare £2000 as being due to Customs and Excise. Suppose that at your next VAT visit it is found that you had missed out a whole page of sales invoices so that another £900 is found to be owing. The correct figure for that tax period is now £2900. £2900 × 30% = £870 so the mistake of £900 is now 'serious' enough for a penalty as it clearly exceeds the figure of £870.

Reasonable Excuse

On the bright side, if you have what is termed a 'reasonable excuse' you might well escape the penalty. On the gloomy side, if someone else made the mistake on your behalf (for example your book-keeper), this does not count as an excuse. Nor does pleading poverty. Anything else might well be worth a try. It is worth noting that the penalty also applies if you put in no VAT return at all and instead pay a centrally issued assessment which is too low.

A Few Words of Advice

The effect all this should have on you is to make you check, double check and triple check everything that goes into each VAT return. With VAT the name of the game is information. If at the end of the day you have even the slightest doubt about what should or should not be included in your VAT return, do not hesitate to ask. You may wish to contact your accountant or you can write to your local VAT office. Do not be shy about asking even the simplest question. After all, it is *your* responsibility to get it right.

Note: *it is much better to get a ruling in writing*. Phone calls might be difficult to prove if you want to use them as evidence. The advantage, of course, with a written ruling from Customs and Excise is that if it turns out to be wrong, it should get you off the hook as far as interest, penalties, and even the original assessment are concerned. If Customs and Excise are not sympathetic you have to go through the route of judicial review or suing the Commissioners for negligence as a VAT tribunal cannot hear cases of misdirection.

2

Sales and Services

When Output Tax is Due – The Tax Point · Tax Invoices · Credits · Bad Debt Relief · Agents · Annual Accounting Scheme · Second-Hand Schemes

When Output Tax is Due – The Tax Point

One of the main problems with supplying goods and services is establishing *when* (that is, in which tax period) output tax on each supply is due to be paid to Customs and Excise. If you get this wrong, not only will Customs and Excise charge you default interest from the time it should have been paid to the time it was actually paid, but possibly a serious misdeclaration penalty as well (see Chapter 1). The time when output tax should be paid to Customs and Excise is called the **tax point**.

If you are a retailer you will be following the rules of whichever retail scheme you are using. These rules are different to the normal rules for traders who issue invoices for their supplies (see Chapter 5: Retail Schemes).

Do not fall into the trap of waiting to be paid for goods and services before accounting for and paying output tax to Customs and Excise. If you wish to pay the output tax when you yourself are paid you must apply to your local VAT office for permission to use the **Cash Accounting scheme**.

Cash Accounting Scheme

This scheme works two ways. You account for the output tax when you yourself are paid. You claim back input tax only when you pay for business purchases and expenses.

However, there are certain conditions to be met before approval is given. The main one is that you do not expect your taxable turnover (do not forget this includes both standard and zero-rated supplies) to exceed a certain limit. At the time of going to press this limit is £300000 over the next 12 months.

The other conditions relate to your history as a VAT registered person. As long as you owe no more than £1000 to Customs and Excise and they are satisfied you will clear any debt outstanding up to this amount, as well as all your returns being up to date, you should be accepted for the scheme.

If your taxable turnover then rises above the £300000 limit you are given a 25% allowance before you have to tell your local VAT office and leave the scheme. So at present your taxable turnover can go up to £375000 before you go over the limit.

If you wish to apply you should obtain Notice 731 'Cash accounting' and fill in the form at the back.

Normal Invoice Traders

For those of you unable to use the Cash Accounting scheme there is no choice but to follow the tax point rules to decide in which period to account for your output tax.

Remember, the tax point is the date when output tax becomes due. There are two tax points. These are (*a*) the basic tax point and (*b*) the actual tax point. The difference between the two is that the basic tax point relates to the date when goods change hands or services are completed, whereas the actual tax point relates to payment received or an invoice issued.

Output tax is usually due at the actual tax point, but if you do not obey the invoicing rules output tax is due instead at the basic tax point. The problem arises if this happens and the two tax points straddle two different tax periods, as this is where default interest and possibly serious misdeclaration penalty could hit you.

The Basic Tax Point

This is the date when goods change hands or services are completed. If you operate mail order, it is the date the goods are sent away. Otherwise it is the date when your customer takes physical possession of the goods.

If you sell somebody something which you install, for example, if you sell a factory a piece of machinery which you take several days to set up, the basic tax point is the date the goods are made available for use.

For services the basic tax point is the date the service is completed.

The Actual Tax Point

Having created a basic tax point, you then have 14 days in which to issue a **tax invoice**. The date the invoice is issued becomes the actual tax point. This is the all-important date on which you have to account for the output tax.

If by some chance you do not issue a tax invoice within 14 days of the basic tax point, the date output tax becomes due reverts to the basic tax point.

This is very important because it means that output tax must be accounted for once a basic tax point has been created. It is no excuse to say that no output tax was accounted for because no invoice was raised.

The only way you can issue a tax invoice more than 14 days after the basic tax point and still account for output tax on its date of issue is if you write to your local VAT office and get their approval.

So if you invoice monthly rather than fortnightly you will need permission from your local VAT office to account for output tax on the date of the invoice.

Other Situations

Unfortunately there are further complications lying in wait for the unwary. An actual tax point is also created if you happen to issue a tax invoice *or* if you are paid *before* the basic tax point. So the date of payment or the invoice date becomes the date when output tax has to be accounted for.

If you issue a tax invoice to cover a payment received before the basic tax point, the actual tax point is the first date of the two – the date of the invoice or the date of payment.

A deposit is normally covered by this so you have to account for output tax as above. But if you take a deposit against the safe return of goods, it is considered that no supply has taken place, so no output tax is due, even if you have to keep the deposit.

If you supply services on a continual basis, the actual tax point is still the date of payment or the date of issue of a tax invoice. If both should happen close together it is whichever comes first, for example, if you issue a tax invoice the day after payment is received.

Although this may sound complicated, do take the time to ensure you understand exactly when you must account for the output tax on each supply. Again, if you have any doubts at all about a particular supply do not hesitate to ask, as you are the one who will have to pay up if you get it wrong.

Cash Flow and Tax Points

The problem for businesses who have to live by the normal tax point rules is that the situation can arise where output tax has to be accounted and paid for a long time (months even) before payment is received. This can lead to severe cash flow problems. This seems to be more acute at times of high interest rates when companies are tempted to hold onto their money for as long as possible before paying their suppliers.

Although Customs and Excise may listen with sympathy to such cases and will point to the Cash Accounting scheme as a solution for small businesses, it is their function to enforce the law so there is no choice but to follow the rules. The only consolation is that if you follow the tax point rules you can reclaim the input tax on your business purchases and expenses on the invoice date, even if you do not pay up for several months (see Chapter 3).

The system works best for those traders who are in a repayment position, like farmers, for example. A farmer with no standard-rate outputs need not worry about accounting for output tax, but can reclaim the input tax on the date of the invoice *and* can have monthly tax periods to get the VAT back even more quickly.

Tax Invoices

The tax invoice is the document which records any supply and as such is one of the most important cogs in the machinery of VAT. It is the evidence needed to reclaim the input tax and, provided the rules outlined in the previous section have been followed, its date of issue dictates the period in which to account for the output tax.

When an officer from the VAT office visits you he or she will want to have a look through your sales and purchase invoices. So it pays to make sure that the tax invoices you issue are correctly filled in and issued at the right time, and that the tax invoices on which you reclaim the VAT are themselves properly constituted tax invoices.

Less Detailed Tax Invoice

In theory a VAT registered person must provide a tax invoice when a supply is made to another VAT registered person. But of course there is no way of telling if someone is VAT registered or not. So in practice you only have to give a tax invoice to a customer if you are asked for one. You can be sure that a VAT registered person will always ask you for one in order to be able to reclaim the input tax.

Retailers form the main group of people who seldom issue full tax invoices (see Chapter 4). Nevertheless, they still have to hand over a tax invoice if asked for one.

However, if you sell something costing £50 or less you can get away with issuing a **less detailed tax invoice**. The good thing about this is that a till receipt will often show all the information required and so will count as a less detailed tax invoice.

Information Required

- Your name, address and VAT registration number.
- The date or tax point.
- The price, including VAT.
- The rate of VAT being applied. You might see on a till slip a code instead of the VAT rate. If this is the case there should also be a key to the code used.

If you sell by credit card you can even adapt the voucher you issue as a less detailed tax invoice. The voucher already shows (or should show) your name, address, the date and the selling price including VAT, so it is simply a case of adding your VAT registration number, the rate of VAT and a description of what is being sold.

Necessary Details

Whenever you issue a tax invoice there is certain information you have to include apart from anything else you may wish to put on it:

- Your own name, address and VAT registration number. This shows that you are indeed VAT registered to the customer who wants to reclaim any VAT.
- Your customer's name and address. Be careful to put the correct details here because your supply might be to your customer, but someone else might pay for it. Only the VAT registered person whose name and address appear here can reclaim the input tax.
- A unique number. This can be a serial number or any other number as long as only that invoice bears that number.
- The tax point or date of issue. Do not forget to follow the tax point rules.

- A description of the type of supply. Is it a straightforward sale, a hire-purchase, on sale or return, on credit, an exchange of goods or a hire of something? Along with this you have to describe what is being sold. If it is goods show how much and what each line costs (excluding VAT). If it is services you have to describe the services, and what has been done for the customer. Every time you describe the supply you also have to include the rate of VAT that is being applied.
- The final price, excluding VAT.
- Any discount offered and how much the discount is (more on this in a moment).
- The VAT itself.
- The total charge, including VAT.

Finally, remember to keep a copy of your sales invoices. Apart from the fact that the law requires you to do so, the copies will help you make up your VAT return (see Chapter 7: Book-keeping and VAT).

Discounts

A few more words about discounts. If you offer your customers discounts you calculate the VAT in different ways according to the type of discount being offered.

Quantity Discount
This is where you offer a discount according to how much is being bought. This one is a straightforward calculation. Before you work out the VAT, simply look at the selling price excluding VAT, calculate the discounted price and then work out the VAT on that figure.

Prompt Payment Discount
This is where you offer your customer a discount provided he or she pays up within a given period of time, for example you may offer a 5% discount if payment is made within 14 days. It is a little more complicated because the VAT amount is worked out on the price the customer would pay if he or she were to take up the discount by paying promptly. Suppose you are offering a prompt payment discount on goods you are selling, and the selling price before VAT is added on is £1000. If the discount is 5% for payment within 14 days you simply work out £1000 – 5% (= £950) and calculate the VAT on the figure you have arrived at (in this case £950 × 17.5% = £166.25). So your tax invoice will show a price before VAT of £1000 and a VAT figure of £166.25.

If you offer a ladder of discounts, for example 7.5% for payment within 1 week, 5% for payment within 2 weeks and 2.5% for payment within 3 weeks, you simply work out the VAT on the greatest discount, in this case on the 7.5%.

A final complication comes if you offer your customer the chance to pay by instalments. In this instance you have to work out the VAT on the amount actually paid. If this is the case and you have problems working out the VAT, to be on the safe side you would be best calculating the VAT on the full selling price, ignoring any discounts. You can always adjust later by issuing a credit note.

Future or Contingent Discounts

These are where you offer a discount based on something else happening, for example if your customer buys more from you at a later date. Since when you sell the goods the discount has not yet been earned, you have to work out the VAT in the normal way on the full selling price. If the customer comes back to buy more later and so gets the discount you have to adjust the VAT by issuing a credit note to reduce your output tax (see page 31).

Disbursements

Care is needed here because VAT law takes a very narrow view of what exactly constitutes a **disbursement** and lays down conditions regarding its treatment. This is perhaps understandable given that no VAT is payable on disbursements. These are that they are shown separately on the tax invoice and the amount charged is exactly the same as the cost of the disbursement. Normally a disbursement is an extra expense borne by somebody else who does work for you which relates only to the work done for you. For example, you might hire a computer expert from the other end of the country to come and set up a new system for you. Apart from paying his or her fee you will also be billed for the travel expenses and any hotel stay necessary. These expenses are over and above the normal service provided and are normally seen as disbursements.

However, as far as VAT is concerned, if you carry out work for a customer and incur extra expenses such as travel tickets, hotel bills, telephone charges and postage etc, these are treated as being part of the supply you make to your customer and are therefore *not* disbursements. This is because, as far as VAT goes, expenses such as these are not supplies to your customer, they are supplies to you.

You can only treat as a disbursement something you arrange on behalf of your customer where the supply effectively by-passes you.

Suppose you arrange to buy a house through your solicitor. His or her services to you, including the incidental expenses incurred on your purchase like telephone and postage costs, form one taxable supply. But when the solicitor pays the stamp duty to the Inland Revenue on your behalf this *is* a disbursement and no VAT is due. Clearly the stamp duty is for your house and not the solicitor's, and the supply by-passes him or her.

Pro Forma Invoices

A **pro forma invoice** is *not* a tax invoice. It is generally used to protect against failure to pay up or is sent in advance of an order. Because a pro forma is not a tax invoice, issuing one does not create a tax point and you cannot reclaim input tax using one as evidence. This is a very important point because if you issue pro formas you should remember to issue a proper tax invoice for each supply (or be prepared to account for output tax at the basic tax point).

You must also write, print or stamp across the pro forma 'This is not a tax invoice' so that the person receiving it knows it is not a proper tax invoice, and that it cannot be used to reclaim input tax. Unfortunately not everyone remembers to put this on their pro formas so do scrutinise all invoices you receive to be on the safe side (see Chapter 3 on purchases).

Self-billing

The **self-billing system** is designed to make life easier for those VAT registered traders who supply goods and services to another VAT registered trader, but where it is only the trader receiving the goods or services who knows how much they cost. It works by the trader who receives the supply issuing the invoice. This one invoice becomes the supplier's sales invoice and the purchase invoice of the trader receiving the supply.

Suppose your business decides to sell a van and to do this you send it off to be auctioned. Clearly you do not know how much the van will fetch until the auctioneer sells it for you. So once it is sold the auctioneers will send you an invoice showing, as all tax invoices should, how much it sold for, the VAT amount and the VAT-inclusive selling price.

Next to the VAT amount the invoice should also say something like 'This is your output tax due to Customs and Excise'. The auctioneer will claim the same figure as his or her input tax. The invoice will also show the auctioneer's commission, since this is the charge from the auctioneer to you and is therefore your input tax and the auctioneer's output tax.

If you want to operate this system yourself you have to write to your local VAT office stating your case. You also have to get the agreement of your suppliers to the self-billing as they cannot issue tax invoices for the supplies in question.

As a supplier yourself you may well come across self-billing as some big companies prefer to operate this system for the measure of control it gives them. The construction industry uses a document called an 'authenticated receipt', issued by the main contractor after deciding on the value of work done by a sub-contractor. This then becomes the sales invoice of the sub-contractor and the purchase invoice of the main contractor.

Part Exchange

When you trade goods in for something else, for example an old van for a new van, it is very important to remember that two separate supplies are taking place; you are effectively selling your old van and being sold a different van. There is a supply *by* you and a supply *to* you.

When you come to record the part exchange in your books you should record the full value of the sale with the output tax and the full value of the purchase with the input tax. This is because there may be a time difference between the two transactions, and where this is the case two different tax periods may be involved. Getting it wrong could then mean default interest and serious misdeclaration penalty (see Chapter 1).

Open Market Value

Output tax is always due on the full or open market value of anything you sell. This prevents people from trying to avoid paying VAT by such schemes as selling a book (zero-rated) for £300 and supplying a television set (standard-rated) for only £1 at the same time. Remember, you still have to account for the full output tax if you barter one thing for another. You have to pay the same amount of output tax as if you had received the whole amount in hard cash.

Finance Companies

These are becoming more popular as they are a useful way for businesses to facilitate sales. When a sale is financed by a finance company there are two supplies taking place: the supplier to the finance company (who becomes the owner of the goods) and the finance company to the customer.

Suppose you decide to buy a van at 0% finance over two years. The garage selling it does all the paperwork and you drive away in it. But the new owner of the van is not you yourself, it is the finance company to whom you pay the instalments. Therefore, in order to reclaim the input tax you will need a tax invoice from the finance company, not from the garage. Similarly the garage will issue the sales invoice to the finance company, not to you.

Credits

When you issue a credit note, for whatever reason, you are reducing the value of the original supply that you made. Naturally Customs and Excise are very interested in anything which reduces the amount of output tax you are due to pay each quarter.

Before you issue a credit note therefore, do make sure that your reason for doing so is valid, i.e. that you are not issuing one merely to avoid having to pay output tax on a supply you have made where payment is unlikely to materialise (for bad debts see the next section). Otherwise issuing credit notes for things like returned goods or a discount earned is of course perfectly acceptable.

The Credit Note

When you make up a credit note you have to include all the information required on a normal tax invoice, but adapt it to show that it is in fact a credit note. Thus, instead of describing the type of supply you have to show the reason for the credit, and the amounts will all be credited sums. The fact that it is so similar to a sales invoice means that if you do not have a supply of specially printed credit notes you can easily adapt a sales invoice for this purpose.

If you and your customers decide between yourselves that adjusting the VAT on a credit note is too much like hard work, you can do this as long as you write something like 'Not a VAT credit note' in big letters across the credit note.

Recording Credit Notes

Remember, when you issue a credit note you are reducing the value of an earlier supply you have made to your customer. So when you enter your credit note in your books you *subtract* the VAT on your credit note from your output tax figure. Most people write a credit note in red in their books to show that it is to be subtracted when the time comes to add up the output tax.

On the other side of the coin, if you yourself receive a credit note because you have been overcharged or are sending goods back, the credit note is now reducing the value of the original supply to you. So you will have to *subtract* the VAT on the credit note from your input tax figure. Again, it is a good idea to use a red pen to make sure you do subtract the VAT when it comes to adding up the figures. Customs and Excise will certainly want to make sure that you have accounted for credit notes both issued and received.

If, once you have adjusted for credit notes, the unusual situation arises where you find you have a minus figure to enter in box 1 or box 2 (output tax and input tax) of your VAT return form, you must write the amount in brackets in the relevant box.

Bad Debt Relief

Not being paid is a sad fact of business life. Having to pay the output tax to Customs and Excise under the normal tax point rules virtually as soon as a supply has been made is an even sadder fact. Retailers and those on the Cash Accounting scheme are of course protected from bad debts automatically by virtue of being able to account for output tax on receipt of payment. Everyone else, however, must follow the system below.

How the System Works

The one good thing about the procedure for reclaiming VAT paid on bad debts is that you do get your money back. Eventually.

The way to go about getting back VAT paid to Customs and Excise on a bad debt is very straightforward. You simply wait one year, write it off in your annual accounts and reclaim the output tax you originally had to pay. Quite how you write it off in your accounts is obviously a matter for your accountant. You should also remember to keep all the documentation relating to the supply which became a bad debt, for example the original invoice(s) and your sales records showing that output tax was indeed originally accounted for.

Having said all this, do not forget to follow the tax point rules as set out in the first section of this chapter. You *cannot* wait for payment before you account for output tax (unless you are a retailer or on the Cash Accounting scheme).

If you do have any bad debts the relevant leaflet is VAT Leaflet 700/18 'Relief from VAT on bad debts'.

Agents

If the situation should arise where you find yourself doing business on behalf of someone else, you would normally be thought of as an **agent**, with the person you are acting for being the **principal**. But when it comes to VAT care is needed, because although you may think yourself an agent for a particular brand or make (as in the motor industry), in cases like this you would trade as a normal business. The supply would be from you to your customer.

To be an agent you are doing business on behalf of someone else, and there are two supplies. There is the supply from the person you represent (your principal) to the final customer, and there is the supply you make to your principal, because naturally you will want to charge him or her for your services in arranging the deal.

Suppose your business acquires a holiday complex of flats in another part of the country. Instead of letting them out yourself you give them to a specialist company to advertise and rent out. Here the two different supplies can readily be identified:

1 Your supply of holiday accommodation to the people who rent them for their holidays (a standard-rated supply)
2 The specialist company's supply of services to your business for its work in letting the properties.

Clearly the specialist company is the agent.

Or, take another example. Suppose your business decides to buy a brand new factory that has just been built and you decide to negotiate and conclude the transaction through your solicitor. Again the two supplies can readily be seen:

1 The supply from the owner of the factory to you
2 The solicitor's supply of services to you in arranging the deal.

As far as VAT goes there are two ways the VAT can be accounted for.

Working Out the VAT

Take the second example above where you decide to buy the factory through your solicitor. The supply of a brand new factory is standard-rated so there are two ways of dealing with the VAT:

1 The seller of the factory 'sells' the factory to the solicitor. He or she issues a sales invoice to the solicitor with output tax shown in the normal way. The solicitor reclaims this as input tax. The solicitor then issues a sales invoice to you showing exactly the same details as the sales invoice to him or her. You then reclaim the output tax shown as your input tax.

   The solicitor has two ways of billing you for his or her services. He or she can either (a) include them on the sales invoice to you but detailing them and the VAT separately or (b) issue you with another tax invoice for his or her services. Do not forget the rules about disbursements if you are the agent. You may in the above example get the solicitor to pay the rates on the factory, which would be a disbursement, but postage, telephone and so on would not (see the earlier section on disbursements).

2 The other way to deal with the VAT is for the seller of the factory to issue a sales invoice direct to you, the buyer, on which you would reclaim the input tax. If the invoice were to pass through the solicitor's hands on its way to you then it would have to remain unaltered. The solicitor is not allowed to change the details if the invoice is made out to him or her, so if this is the case then you have to go through the first procedure (see above). The solicitor then issues an invoice to you for services rendered.

If you are the agent it is important to remember that you must account for the VAT on each supply. Do not offset the charge for your own services against money you receive for your principal when you make out the invoice(s). Although in the end the result may be the same, if a tax period were to interrupt the two supplies you could risk default interest and serious misdeclaration penalty. Examples of businesses which act as agents include estate agents, private investigators, employment agencies and, of course, auctioneers.

Annual Accounting Scheme

Annual Accounting is the other scheme for small businesses apart from the Cash Accounting scheme. It is designed for those who find filling in a quarterly VAT return too much hard work and worry. As with the Cash Accounting scheme there are certain conditions.

The Annual Accounting scheme works by you making 9 monthly payments to Customs and Excise by direct debit. You pay the tenth instalment by completing an annual return which will show how much you are outstanding for the year, or how much you have overpaid and can claim back.

Obviously the main advantage is that you only have to fill in one VAT return per year. And Customs and Excise give you an extra month to complete your return. However, the conditions are similar to those imposed on the Cash Accounting scheme. You apply on the form in Notice 732 'Annual accounting': again the taxable turnover limit is £300 000, and again you can take this up to £375 000 before you have to leave the scheme. Your local VAT office will decide the amount you pay on each of the 9 direct debit instalments by looking at your past year's VAT returns and estimating accordingly.

This scheme is only for those traders who pay tax rather than reclaim tax each quarter. If you are a repayment trader you will have to continue with your monthly or quarterly returns.

By reducing the number of returns you have to submit you will, of course, reduce the risk of incurring default interest and serious misdeclaration penalty.

Second-hand Schemes

Until now it has been stressed that VAT is due on the full, or open market value of any supply you may make. However, as with most rules, there are exceptions to this one and these exceptions relate exclusively to those businesses which deal in certain second-hand goods. These are: cars, antiques and works of art (including collectors' pieces), motorbikes, caravans, boats and outboard motors, aircraft, electronic organs, firearms and horses.

The **second-hand schemes** were designed to help second-hand dealers, and perhaps it is because of this that they are not compulsory. They work quite simply. An item is bought and then it is sold. Instead of the normal rules being applied where VAT is due on the full selling price, under these schemes output tax is calculated on the difference, or margin, between the buying price and the selling price.

If you are a second-hand car dealer who buys a car for £1000 and sells it on for £2000 then output tax is due, not on the £2000 selling price but only on the margin, which is £2000 − £1000 = £1000 (multiply by 7 and divide by 47 to get the output tax due). And, if you happen to sell it for less than you paid for it then no output tax is due at all on the supply. Of course if you do use any of the second-hand schemes, you cannot reclaim input tax on any goods bought in to be sold under a particular second-hand scheme.

Conditions

In order to be able to buy and sell goods under any of the second-hand schemes you have to stick to the conditions laid down by Customs and Excise. If you do not you may have to revert to the normal rules and account for output tax on the full selling price, which could be an expensive process if a visiting officer applies the normal rules retrospectively so that you end up paying a lot of back tax. Then, of course, there is always default interest and serious misdeclaration penalty looming in the background.

There are three basic conditions for buying and selling goods under these schemes:

1 No tax invoice is issued *to* you
2 No tax invoice is issued *by* you
3 You obey all the rules about which records to keep.

You have to record everything in much greater detail than ordinary traders. When you buy an article you must have a purchase invoice (*not* a tax invoice), so if you buy from an ordinary member of the public you have to make a purchase invoice yourself. This must still show the name and address of the seller together with your name and address. It has to have a unique number, the date and a detailed description of the goods. It differs from a normal tax invoice in that no VAT registration numbers are shown and the only price is the one paid. The procedure is similar when you sell the article. You make out a sales invoice with your name, address and VAT registration number, the name and address of the buyer, the unique number, the date, the description and the total price. The additional details required vary from scheme to scheme so do consult the leaflets (see below).

Somewhere on both the purchase and sales invoices a stock book reference number should be recorded in addition to everything else. This is because for each scheme you have to keep a detailed stock book which records every conceivable detail of each and every transaction. It records all the purchase details including the invoice number, the sales details including the invoice number as well as the margin, the tax rate and the VAT due to Customs and Excise. The number of columns needed in the stock book to record all this ranges from 13 to 15 depending on which scheme you are using, with a special scheme for horses and ponies (see below). You can make up your own stock book or obtain one produced by the relevant trade association.

The 9 Second-hand Schemes

1 'Second-hand Cars' Notice 711

This notice comes with a handy red pull-out section telling you exactly what records to keep – well worth reading because it is one of the few leaflets which can be understood without sub-cranial tension and confusion. (Cars are themselves a whole problem area on their own as far as VAT is concerned and are dealt with in detail in Chapter 8: Problem Areas.)

If you buy a second-hand car from a dealer then it will almost certainly be sold to you under the scheme. Note the word 'car': only second-hand cars, not vans or lorries, can be bought and sold in this way. Vans, lorries, pick-ups and so on all have to be dealt with under the normal VAT rules. A car is defined as a passenger vehicle with more than 1 and less than 12 seats, so some of the bigger 'people carriers' count too.

Something to watch out for when you operate the scheme is if you sell a car with a tax disc. Where this occurs it is part of the supply so output tax is due on the full margin. But if you obtain the tax disc on behalf of your customer then this counts as a disbursement so you do not include it in the margin.

2 'Works of Art, Antiques and Collectors' Pieces' Notice 712

This one too comes with a handy pull-out section, this time in a tasteful shade of yellow ochre probably meant by Customs and Excise to resemble the sepia tint of old photographs. Again it provides very clear information on the records that have to be kept and how they are to be filled in. However, having been pleasantly surprised to find that the official literature can be understood you will then discover that the law on VAT defines works of art, antiques and collectors' pieces completely differently to any other definition of what they constitute. So before assuming that what you are selling, or are planning to sell, falls under, or will fall under, this scheme do make sure you check first.

(a) Works of art

This includes a painting or drawing in whatever medium, be it oils, pastels, water colours or gouache, hand-produced engravings or etchings, sculptures or carvings. Not included is pottery, ceramics or mosaics (which you may well think odd), photographic lithographs and commercial ornaments.

(b) Antiques

An antique has to be more than 100 years old to fulfil Customs and Excise requirements. So if you have what you think is an antique which is only 99 years old you have no choice but to wait another year if you want it to qualify for the scheme. Excluded are loose gems (including pearls) but interestingly you can include them in the scheme if they are strung together as a necklace.

(c) Collectors' pieces

These cover objects of interest to museums, for example stuffed animals, mineral specimens, skeletons, fossils, archaeological finds and pre-World War 1 medals. If you cannot decide whether something can be included or not then the best thing to do is to ask.

3 'Second-hand caravans and motor caravans' Notice 717

The definition here of what can be included in the scheme is strictly limited to the trailer and motor caravan.

4 'Second-hand motorcycles' Notice 713

This is the scheme for motorbikes, scooters, mopeds and, curiously, any other one-seater vehicle. So a one-person bubble car would be sold under this scheme and not under the second-hand cars scheme.

5 'Second-hand boats and outboard motors' Notice 720

This scheme also covers yachts, canoes and sailboards.

6 'Second-hand aircraft' Notice 721

This is a broadly defined scheme. If it is a machine and it flies you can sell it under this scheme, as it includes machines without engines such as gliders and hang gliders.

7 'Second-hand electronic organs' Notice 722

Note that this scheme is for electronic organs only. It does not include the manual organ which uses a pump instead of human effort.

8 'Second-hand firearms' Notice 724

9 'Second-hand horses and ponies' Notice 726

The record keeping requirements of this scheme are very strict, and you must use the form issued by the British Equestrian Trade Association.

Remember, these are all second-hand schemes so the first sale of any item will not apply.

3

Purchases

What Input Tax Can Be Reclaimed?

When you buy something for your business you are almost certain to be charged VAT. As a VAT registered person you can reclaim this VAT as long as it relates to goods and services for your business, both expenses *of* the business and purchases *for* the business.

If you make taxable *and* exempt supplies you might not be able to reclaim all the VAT on your business purchases and expenses, but the next chapter (Chapter 4: Partial Exemption) deals with this in some detail.

Inevitably there are complications in reclaiming VAT even if the only supplies you make are taxable – either standard and/or zero-rated. It is important to remember here that Customs and Excise and the Inland Revenue are entirely separate, so that what you can reclaim VAT on and what you can claim against the Inland Revenue are *not* one and the same.

Although you can reclaim the VAT on most business purchases and expenses there are exceptions and you should be aware of these when filling in your VAT return. See the section on page 43.

Evidence Needed

Before going any further it is important to note that you need a tax invoice in order to reclaim the VAT. Have a look back at the section on tax invoices in the previous chapter so you know what has to be included on an invoice to make it a proper tax invoice.

It has to be made out to you with your name and address as you are the person receiving the supply. It does not matter that someone else might be paying, because if the supply is to you, you are the only person who can reclaim the input tax. So if you have two or three associated businesses, input tax can only be reclaimed by the business receiving the supply even though another might pay for it.

The other major hazard to beware of is the invoice without a VAT registration number on it. Lack of one means your supplier is not VAT registered, in which case there is no VAT charged, and no VAT to be reclaimed. Also beware of pro forma invoices, as these are not proper tax invoices.

When No Evidence is Needed

Having said that you must always have a tax invoice to reclaim the VAT on business purchases and expenses, there are a few minor exceptions. If you find yourself having to pay out for car parking, telephone calls or vending machine purchases you can still reclaim the VAT you paid even though you have no evidence to support your claim.

You have to be certain that the supplier is VAT registered and there is a limit of £25 which is applied to what you spend. So if you pay out £25 for parking your car at an airport while you go away on a business trip you can reclaim the VAT, but any more and you would not be able to. A word of warning – parking meters do not charge VAT so do not try to reclaim VAT on money you feed into them.

Types of Supply

Remember, input tax can be reclaimed on most business purchases and expenses (including imports, see Chapter 6: Imports and Exports). Before going any further it will be useful to look at the different types of supply and how they affect input tax.

Taxable Supplies

If you make standard and/or zero-rated supplies you can reclaim the VAT on most of your business purchases and expenses and this should be a fairly straightforward process. For example, if you have a shop you will reclaim the VAT on your goods bought in for resale as well as on incidental expenses like telephone bills or the purchase of a new van. If you are a service industry you will reclaim VAT on your expenses.

Whilst on the subject of expenses, you can reclaim the VAT on any subsistence expenses like hotel bills and meals as long as they are taken far enough away from your home and business addresses to be considered necessary expenses. You cannot reclaim VAT on these locally. Expenses are an exception to the rule about tax invoices being made out to you as the VAT registered person. As a VAT registered person you can still reclaim the VAT if the tax invoices are made out to your employees instead of to you, whether for hotel and meal bills away from home and work, or for petrol or diesel used for business purposes.

Exempt Supplies

This is a problem area and Chapter 4 is devoted exclusively to it. Basically you cannot reclaim the VAT on purchases and expenses relating to exempt supplies. However, if you make exempt *and* taxable supplies you can reclaim the related input tax up to certain limits (see Chapter 4: Partial Exemption).

Outside the Scope

You cannot reclaim VAT on any purchases to be used for making supplies which are outside the scope of United Kingdom VAT. So you cannot, for example, reclaim the VAT relating to supplies not made in the course of business (charities are the main ones affected here) or hobbies. Also outside the scope are racehorse winnings so you could not reclaim the VAT on a racehorse to be used for racing.

The problem with outside the scope income, especially in a case like that of a charity where input tax can relate to both taxable and non-business activities (for example input tax on general overheads), is to work out what proportion of the input tax can be reclaimed. A calculation like those shown in Chapter 4 has to be done to split the input tax.

Pre-registration VAT

You may well have had to pay VAT on business purchases and expenses before you were registered, for example on stock or on accountant's bills. As far as goods are concerned you can reclaim the VAT as long as you have a tax invoice and you still possess the goods in question once registered for VAT.

Services are slightly different. You can only reclaim the VAT incurred on services for setting up the business up to 6 months before registration. Do not forget to keep all the evidence so that Customs and Excise can see that these conditions have been met.

What You Cannot Reclaim VAT On

Having said that you can reclaim VAT on most business purchases and expenses there are a few exceptions. Do keep an eye out for input tax on the following purchases and expenses and do remember *not* to reclaim the VAT.

Cars
You cannot reclaim the VAT on a car. The only exception to this is a car dealer. Otherwise not even a driving school or a taxi company can reclaim the VAT on the purchase of a car. Customs and Excise define a car as being a passenger vehicle with all round windows and more than 1 seat but less than 12 seats. (There is a section on cars in Chapter 8: Problem Areas because claiming back the VAT on petrol or diesel and leases is such a complicated business.)

Personal spending
Remember, input tax can only be reclaimed on business expenditure, so you cannot go along to the cash and carry, stock up with goodies for your home and reclaim the VAT.

One area to consider carefully is VAT incurred on mixed business/personal expenditure. You might run your business from home and use your telephone mostly for business. But before you reclaim the VAT on your telephone bill you will have to apportion, or split it, because Customs and Excise know that at least some of the calls made on the telephone will be personal rather than business ones.

This is where confusion about Customs and Excise and the Inland Revenue may cause problems. Although you may have agreed a split bill with the Inland Revenue, you have not agreed anything with Customs and Excise unless you have talked to them separately. Once you have agreed a split with Customs and Excise, simply write on the bill the percentage you are to claim and the amount of money this represents, for example 75% of a £10 bill claimed = £7.50 claimed.

Another example of VAT incurred on mixed expenditure is where your home and office are in one building and you wish to reclaim input tax on repairs to the roof.

Again, a split will have to be agreed with Customs and Excise.

Business entertainment
It does not matter if you get a contract out of taking the managing director of another company to restaurants, nightclubs, the races or football matches – you cannot reclaim the VAT on business entertainment.

Anything bought from a dealer under one of the second-hand schemes
The dealer is not allowed to give you a tax invoice anyway because he or she is only accounting for output tax on the margin, or difference, between the selling price and the purchase price. See Chapter 2 for these schemes.

Certain articles installed in a new house
Obviously this applies in the main to builders. VAT cannot be reclaimed on anything which is not classed as an essential fixture or fitting (for example carpets, washing machines and so on). The relevant leaflet is 708/2 'Construction Industry'.

When to Reclaim Input Tax

In Chapter 2, when output tax on sales and services was discussed, it was stressed that you must account for output tax at the correct time, and that failure to do so might lead to trouble with default interest and possibly serious misdeclaration penalty. These can also hit you if you make mistakes with your input tax, for example if you claim back too much input tax in error or if you reclaim the VAT on something in the above list.

Timing your Input Tax

Apart from ensuring that you have a tax invoice for each purchase and that you are not reclaiming input tax on forbidden items, you should also make sure that you do not fall into the trap of reclaiming input tax too early. If you are on the Cash Accounting scheme, remember that because you do not have to account for and pay output tax until you yourself are paid, you cannot reclaim input tax until you actually pay your bills.

For those of you operating under the normal tax point rules the system works to your advantage. This is because you can claim back the input tax on the invoice date (the supplier's tax point), even though you may wait weeks or even months to pay that bill.

If you are reclaiming VAT on the invoice date, do take care to ensure that when you come to fill in your VAT return you are only claiming input tax on invoices which belong by date reference to that period.

Suppose your tax period runs to 31 October. Suppose that on 1 November you go out and buy a brand new van for the business and get a tax invoice dated for that day, 1 November. Now you have until the end of November to fill in your VAT return which ended on 31 October. Suppose that, without thinking, you put the invoice for the van (dated 1 November) into the VAT return ending 31 October. If you fail to spot your mistake and correct it (see Chapter 7 for correcting errors you discover), a visiting VAT officer will send you an assessment to bring the invoice forward into the right tax period. You will then incur default interest and perhaps serious misdeclaration penalty. So do keep an eye on the dates of your invoices when you come to enter them in your books.

Reclaiming Input Tax Later

If, for some reason, you do not reclaim input tax as soon as you are able to (for example if you lose an invoice), simply reclaim it in a later period. Customs and Excise do not mind if you do not claim back money, as it means they can keep hold of it longer!

Do beware of attempting to combat default interest and serious misdeclaration penalty by deliberately not reclaiming some input tax each tax period. You may hope that this will have the effect of reducing any mistakes found later by putting these invoices back into the tax periods in which they originally belonged, thus avoiding default interest and serious misdeclaration penalty. However, unfortunately this does not work because input tax 'belongs' only to the period in which it is actually claimed, and no other. So any outstanding invoices can only be included in your next VAT return. They cannot be put back into any other tax period.

The best thing to do is to reclaim input tax as soon as you are entitled to. After all, it is money due to you. If you find some unclaimed tax invoices put them in your next VAT return. However, if you do find yourself reclaiming large amounts like this you may get a visit from the VAT office to see what is going on.

Reclaiming VAT Paid in Other EC Countries

Because VAT is a European tax you will have to pay VAT when you visit other EC countries, just as you do in this country. However, there is a special scheme whereby you can reclaim the VAT on expenses and business purchases made in Europe.

This scheme applies only to incidental expenses. It does not cover exports which are zero-rated anyway (see Chapter 6: Imports and Exports). Incidental expenses would be incurred by visiting a trade fair, for example, where you might hire a car and buy some samples on which you have to pay VAT.

The way the scheme works is that you have to keep the tax invoice and apply to the relevant public body in the country where you paid the VAT. Each country has different rules, for example they all have different upper and lower monetary limits for using the scheme, so you will need to get hold of Notice 723 'Refunds of VAT in the European Community and other countries' from your local VAT office. This gives you the addresses to write to and the precise conditions laid down by each country. An added complication is that you have to apply in the language of the country in question, but you can authorise an agent to do this for you.

4

Input Tax and Exempt Supplies – Partial Exemption

Introduction · Exempt Supplies · The Business Simplification Test · Standard and Special Methods of Calculation · The De Minimis Test · Capital Goods Scheme · The Clawback · Self-supply of Stationery

Introduction

If you only make taxable supplies, either standard-rated or zero-rated, you can reclaim most of your input tax which relates to those supplies. There are only the normal restrictions on what you can and cannot claim (see Chapter 3). But, if any of the supplies you make are exempt, you have to look at your input tax each tax period and relate it to your exempt supplies. This is because exempt supplies are not taxable – they are exempt from VAT. So in theory you cannot reclaim the input tax which relates to exempt supplies. If you only make exempt supplies you cannot register for VAT.

The Theory of Partial Exemption

Obviously you are only affected by partial exemption if you make both taxable *and* exempt supplies. Being partially exempt means just that, i.e. some of your input tax relates to exempt supplies, which in turn means you cannot reclaim this VAT.

However, in order to keep as many people as possible from being partially exempt, Customs and Excise have set certain limits – called the **de minimis** limits. If your exempt input tax, i.e. your input tax which relates to the exempt supplies you make, goes over these limits then you become partially exempt, in which case you cannot reclaim your exempt input tax. If your exempt input tax stays below these de minimis limits you stay **fully taxable**, which means you can reclaim all your input tax as normal, even though some of it relates to exempt supplies. You are treated as if you only make taxable supplies.

This may sound complicated (indeed it is probably the most complex area of VAT that exists), but remember that if you are finding it difficult everyone else is too. Follow it through slowly, make sure you understand how it relates to your particular situation, and, if you run into even the slightest doubt, do not hesitate to ask at your local VAT office. Remember, it is *your* VAT return and *you*, and you alone, are responsible for getting it right.

The first thing to do is to get hold of Notice 706 'Partial exemption' from your local VAT office. You might find this heavy going but it is an important document to refer to once you understand what is going on.

Exempt Supplies

Before going into partial exemption it is important to establish exactly which supplies are exempt. VAT Leaflet 701/39 'VAT liability law' is useful here because it reproduces the law about which supplies are exempt and which are zero-rated.

Here are the main areas of exempt supplies.

Land and Property

This is a very complex area of liability. If you are involved in land, property and/or construction it is vitally important that you are clear about the liability of your supplies. The publications covering this area are Notices 742 (A and B) 'Property development' and 'Property ownership', and Leaflets 708/2 'Construction industry' and 708/1 'Protected buildings'.

Further complications are provided by the **option to tax**. This applies only to the renting or leasing of commercial property and means that you can, if you wish, change the liability of some exempt supplies from exempt to standard-rated. On the plus side you can then reclaim all the input tax which relates to those supplies, which could be handy if you are contemplating major repairs or renovations. On the minus side, once you have opted to tax by writing to your local VAT office telling them of your decision, you have made an irreversible choice. This might cause problems if later the VAT you have to charge cannot be totally reclaimed because your customer is partially exempt. Here is a summary of liabilities:

Standard-rated

- Construction services to commercial buildings and civil engineering works (including demolition)
- Supply of a new* commercial or industrial building
- Surrender of an interest in, or right over, land
- **Self-supply** of construction services
- Supply of land with new civil engineering works.

Zero-rated

- Construction services to new dwellings, residential or community projects
- Approved alterations to listed buildings
- Supply of listed buildings to be used for dwellings, residential or community use which have been substantially reconstructed
- Supply of a new dwelling, residential or community project.

Exempt

- Supply of old commercial buildings, including listed buildings (with option to tax)
- Supply of land with old civil engineering works (with option to tax)
- Supply of old dwellings (*no* option to tax)
- Supply of listed buildings (with option to tax)
- Supply of land (with option to tax)
- Domestic rents (*no* option to tax)
- Commercial rents (with option to tax).

* New = 3 years from the time of completion.

Finance and Insurance

If you make money from money your supply may well be exempt. The relevant publication is VAT Leaflet 701/29 'Finance'. This mainly affects banks, building societies, finance companies, stock exchange brokers and so on. However, if you sell through a finance company, any commission you receive is exempt.

As far as insurance goes, the provisions here really only apply to the insurance business. The relevant leaflet is 701/36 'Insurance'.

Education

Most supplies of education are exempt. Obviously universities and schools are the main bodies concerned, although if you give private tuition you are also making an exempt supply. Curiously, if you teach under contract to a school your supply is no longer exempt. The leaflet you will need is 701/30 'Education'.

'Betting and Gaming'

The main point to remember here is that although your takings from betting and gaming are exempt, admission charges and gaming machine takings are always standard-rated. See VAT Leaflet 701/26.

Postage

Selling stamps is an exempt supply. If, however, you sell them for more than the amount shown on the stamp you have to account for output tax on the difference. Delivery charges are a little more tricky. If, when you sell something, you charge extra for delivery, you have to account for output tax on the delivery charge. This is because only the Post Office can make an exempt supply of delivery. However, if you have a mail order business where it is assumed that goods and delivery are bought together, the liability of the delivery charge follows that of the goods you are selling. So children's clothing sold through mail order will make the delivery charge zero-rated as well.

Health

The liability of your supply here depends on whether you are a registered practitioner, and what type of treatment is being offered. Orthodox treatment by a registered practitioner is exempt, while any alternative treatment, or treatment by someone not registered, is standard-rated. The publication is VAT Leaflet 701/31 'Health'.

Funeral Services

Most supplies in this area are exempt. However, pet funerals are standard-rated, as are the incidental items like inscriptions and newspaper advertisements. VAT Leaflet 701/32 'Burial and cremation' is the relevant publication.

'Trade Unions, Professional Bodies and Learned Societies'

This is the title of VAT Leaflet 701/33. The main point to remember if you are involved in any of these bodies is that the sale of goods such as ties, mugs and clothes are standard-rated, as well as admission charges for non-members.

'Competitions in Sport and Physical Recreation', VAT Leaflet 701/34

This is actually quite complicated as the liability depends very much on the status of the body organising the competitions and the competitors taking part.

'Sales of Antiques, Works of Art etc. from Stately Homes'

This is the title of VAT Leaflet 701/12. Basically the supply here is exempt as long as the sale is exempt from capital taxes.

The Business Simplification Test

The first thing to do is to look at your present and future income to see if any of it comes, or will come, from exempt supplies.

The next step is to identify the input tax which relates to this exempt supply or supplies. Remember, the whole point of this exercise is to see whether or not you can be classed as fully taxable, and thus able to reclaim all your input tax, when you come to fill in your VAT return.

Future Exempt Supplies

You have to go through this process from the very first VAT return in which you incur input tax which relates to exempt supplies (exempt input tax). Suppose you decide as a business venture to do up an old house for resale (an exempt supply). It might take you a year to complete this project, but from the moment you start buying in materials and services for that house, you start to incur exempt input tax. So from that time on you have to work out your partial exemption position every time you come to do your VAT return.

Input Tax You Can Ignore – The Test Itself

Before you start to calculate anything, do the business simplification test by having a look at the following list. If any of your input tax relates to these supplies, you can ignore it *vis-à-vis* partial exemption and simply reclaim it.

- Letting or leasing property. There are two conditions here. Firstly, that the related input tax is less than £1000 in any tax year (the tax year runs to the end of March, April or May depending on your VAT returns). Secondly, that any other exempt input tax you have relates only to supplies in this list. So if all you do is rent out the flat above your shop you do not have to worry about the input tax on repairs, etc. until it reaches £1000 in any tax year.
- Assigning a debt
- Arranging credit (including hire-purchase and conditional sales)
- Arranging mortgages
- Arranging insurance
- Taking deposits

The reason for this test is that the related input tax is very small. Suppose you are an estate agent, and that your normal taxable supplies are selling properties on behalf of clients. Suppose you also arrange mortgages for people who buy property through your estate agency. Now the commission you would receive for this is exempt. But working out the related input tax would just be a nuisance. There would be a proportion of the telephone bill, any repairs, etc. and the amount would not be much at all. So you can simply ignore it and reclaim it.

Businesses Which Cannot Ignore this Input Tax

Having just said that you can ignore the input tax relating to the above list, not everybody can. If whatever you do in the above list grows to such an extent that it could be considered a separate business, then you *cannot* ignore the related input tax. You have to do the calculation set out in the next section and include this input tax in it.

This means that businesses such as banks, building societies, insurance companies or agents, mortgage brokers, finance companies and so on have to abide by the normal rules and do the partial exemption calculation each tax period. So if, as an estate agent, you find that your mortgage broking activities start to take over from your taxable supplies you will have to be careful not to be caught out. The best thing to do would be to write to your local VAT office asking them when they would consider your mortgage broking to be a separate business activity.

Standard and Special Methods of Calculation

So you have reached the stage of having identified your exempt supplies, or supply. If you have failed the business simplification test you will have to go on to the calculation to determine your exact position with regard to partial exemption.

However, if you incur exempt input tax on the letting or leasing of property, you will still need some method of working out if and when the input tax on your repairs exceeds the £1000 limit. This should present few problems if the property in question is entirely separate, such as a detached house. The problem comes if, for example, you rent out the flat above your shop. Suppose the roof covering both the flat and the shop needs major repair work. In this case you will need to use the calculation on page 54 to work out how much input tax relates to the flat and how much to the shop.

Sorting Out Your Input Tax

Before going any further you should put aside all the input tax which you cannot reclaim anyway. This includes input tax relating to non-business activities as well as input tax on items like cars and business entertainment (see Chapter 3 for the full list).

Having put this input tax to one side you are left with three types of input tax:

1 Directly attributable exempt input tax
All the input tax which relates exclusively to your exempt supplies goes under this heading. In the example of the flat above the shop it will be things like repairs to the flat or new double glazing for the windows, etc.

2 Directly attributable taxable input tax
All the input tax which relates only to your taxable supplies goes into this group. Remember, taxable supplies include both zero- and standard-rated supplies. In the example of the shop it will include the input tax on goods bought in for onward sale, repairs to the shop itself and the telephone bill, etc.

3 Input tax which relates to both taxable* and *exempt supplies
This is called your **non-attributable input tax** because you cannot

split it. In the example the input tax on the roof repairs, which cover both the shop and the flat, is the non-attributable input tax.

Recording This Input Tax

If you incur all three types of input tax you will need three columns in your book to record them. Doing this will make life so much simpler when your tax period comes to an end and you have to work out your partial exemption position. The whole reason for the next part, the calculation, is to split your non-attributable input tax to find out what proportion of it relates to exempt supplies. Then you can see if you have exceeded the de minimis limits to find out whether or not you can reclaim all your input tax.

Standard Method of Calculation

For this calculation there is just one more sifting process to go through. This is because the **standard method** is based on inputs (if you want to use outputs you have to use a special method). The idea is to get as accurate a result as possible, so anything which might distort the picture is removed.

You should therefore put aside any input tax you incur from the following list:

- Input tax on any self-supply you make. This includes construction services and stationery (see the last section in this chapter).
- Input tax on capital goods. These capital goods are computers, land and buildings of more than a certain value. More on this later.
- Input tax on any supply to you where you are acting as an agent (see Chapter 2).
- Input tax on any goods bought for resale under a supply of finance. This will only affect you if you lend money, for example if you are a finance company buying in a lorry to sell under a hire-purchase agreement.

As you can see, this is a fairly specialised list so the chances are that none of it will apply to you.

The Calculation Itself

The standard method is merely a calculation to work out what proportion of your inputs relate to taxable supplies. You can in fact use any calculation you like based on this, but the one generally used is done on input tax:

$$\frac{\text{Input tax relating only to taxable supplies}}{\text{Total input tax}} = \text{Proportion of your non-attributable input tax which relates to taxable supplies}$$

You now have a figure with which to work out your total exempt input tax. You simply multiply the figure you got from the above calculation by your non-attributable input tax. This gives you your taxable input tax. Simply subtract this figure from the total non-attributable input tax figure and you have the exempt input tax figure. Add this to the rest of your exempt input tax and you have a total exempt input tax figure.

Example

Suppose you own a hi-fi shop from which you sell music systems and accessories. These are standard-rated. Suppose you also sell them through a finance company for which you get commission, which is exempt. Suppose you also own the flat above the shop which you rent to a family, also an exempt supply.

The three groups of input tax are:

1 Directly attributable exempt input tax. This will be repairs to the flat as well as any general maintenance work done to it.
  Suppose in the first tax period this input tax came to £1500.
2 Directly attributable taxable input tax. This will be hi-fi equipment for onward sale as well as the accessories.
  Suppose in the first tax period this input tax came to £6000.
3 Non-attributable input tax. This will be repairs to the roof covering both the shop and the flat as well as any general overheads.
  Suppose in the first tax period this input tax came to £500.

Because the input tax which relates to the rent of the flat clearly exceeds the £1000 limit set by the business simplification test, you will have to do the calculation to find your total exempt input tax:

$$\frac{£6000}{£8000} = \text{0.75 which is then multiplied by the non-attributable figure of £500 to give £375}$$

So £375 = the proportion relating to taxable supplies.

£500 – £375 = £125, which is the proportion relating to exempt supplies.

The other exempt input tax was £1500 (see above), so £1500 + £125 = £1625.

£1625 is therefore your total exempt input tax.

Special Method of Calculation

A **special method** can be any other method you can think of to work out your total exempt input tax. If you think that the standard method is not giving you a fair result or is too difficult to operate then you should consider a special method. A calculation based on outputs is a special method:

$$\frac{\text{Value of taxable outputs}}{\text{Value of total outputs}} = \begin{array}{l}\text{Proportion of your non-attributable input tax}\\ \text{which relates to taxable supplies}\end{array}$$

You have to have the approval of your local VAT office to use this method, or any other method that best suits your accounting. They want to make sure that the calculation you use is not going to distort the result in your favour. In fact you would be well advised to write to them regardless of the method you decide on, just to make sure.

The De Minimis Test

The next step, having done the calculation, is to see whether you are within the de minimis limits.

If your exempt input tax is

(*a*) Less than an average of £100 a month
(*b*) Less than an average of £250 a month *and* less than 50% of all your input tax
(*c*) Less than an average of £500 a month *and* less than 25% of all your input tax

then you remain fully taxable and you can reclaim this input tax. If your exempt input tax goes over these limits you become partially exempt, so you cannot reclaim this input tax.

Example
Going back to the hi-fi shop, at the end of the first period the total exempt input tax came to £1625, against a total input tax figure of £8000.

At this point the de minimis test has to be applied. Now the hi-fi shop is a normal payment trader and so fills in a VAT return every three months. So the test is applied at follows:

(*a*) £1625 is clearly greater than £100 a month so fails part 1
(*b*) £1625 is also greater than £250 a month so fails part 2
(*c*) £1625 is also greater than £500 a month so fails part 3

So at the end of the first tax period you are partially exempt and cannot reclaim the exempt input tax.

This test has to be done at the end of each tax period up to the end of the tax year. When the end of the tax year is reached (the return ending March, April or May) the **annual adjustment** has to be carried out.

Annual Adjustment

The purpose of this is to look at your whole year to see if you are partially exempt or fully taxable for the whole year, to take account of any fluctuations. It has to be done at the end of the tax year which is the return ending March, April or May, depending on when your tax periods end. For monthly tax periods it is the return ending March. It is simply a case of doing the calculation and applying the de minimis limits for the whole year's figures.

Example

Returning to the hi-fi shop, at the end of the first period the de minimis test had been failed and you were partially exempt. Suppose, however, that in the next tax period you turn the flat into a shop storeroom, so that exempt supply ceases. But you still have to do the annual adjustment.

Remember, the exempt input tax for that one period was £1625 and the total input tax was £8000. Suppose the rest of the year's input tax came to £6000, giving a total input tax figure of £14000. The situation now changes drastically because the whole year's input tax is being considered.

(*a*) £1625 is still greater than £100 a month so fails part 1
(*b*) £1625 is *less* than £250 a month on average (£250 × 12 months = £3000) *and* less than 50% of all your input tax (which is £14000)

So now you have become fully taxable for the year because you have passed the de minimis test for the whole year.

Adjusting Your Return

If, as in the above example, your situation changes from being partially exempt to fully taxable at the end of the tax year, you have to adjust your input tax. The hi-fi shop should reclaim the input tax not originally reclaimed at the end of the first tax period. This is done in the next VAT return after the end of tax year calculation.

Capital Goods Scheme

This scheme really only applies to the larger business. It applies to:

- Any computer you buy which costs more than £50000, excluding VAT
- Any land and buildings costing more than £250000, excluding VAT.

Basically, you review the type of supply the computer or the land and buildings are used for over a set number of years. If the supply changes from being taxable to exempt or vice versa, you have to adjust the amount of input tax you can claim accordingly. For computers this period is 5 years, for land and buildings it is 10 years. In the year you make the purchase you have to include the input tax in the calculation as appropriate (see the previous section). In subsequent years you adjust the input tax you reclaimed as appropriate, as and if the use to which they are put changes from exempt to taxable, and vice versa. The relevant leaflet is 706/2 'Capital goods scheme'.

The Clawback

If you reclaim input tax for an intended taxable supply, and then change that supply to an exempt one, Customs and Excise will take the input tax back. This is of course assuming you end up partially exempt and not fully taxable. It works the other way too, so if you did not reclaim input tax because it was not for a taxable supply, and then change the supply to a taxable one, you can ask for the input tax back.

An example of this would be if you started building a house (zero-rated when sold) and reclaimed the relevant input tax. If you then changed your mind and decided to rent it out instead of selling it, you would have to repay the input tax, as domestic rents are an exempt supply.

Self-supply of Stationery

If you are partially exempt and you produce your own stationery, you have to charge yourself output tax on the standard-rated stationery you produce. How much of it you can reclaim again depends on your partial exemption position. The reason for this is that printing firms would be at an unfair disadvantage by having to charge you VAT. If you could not reclaim all of this because you are partially exempt you might be tempted to produce it yourself. Hence the rule preventing you saving any VAT by producing stationery yourself. VAT Leaflets 701/10 'Printed and similar matter' and 706/1 'Self-supply of stationery' explain the scheme.

5

Retail Schemes

Introduction · The Daily Gross Take · The Retail Schemes · Retail Exports

Introduction

As a retailer you will not want to fill in a tax invoice for each and every sale you make, especially as most of your sales will probably be to the general public who will neither want nor expect one. If a VAT registered person asks you for a proper tax invoice you will have to give one to him or her for input tax deduction, but as a rule you will measure your sales in terms of money received. Customs and Excise, recognising this, set up the retail schemes to enable you to work out your output tax on this basis rather than making you go through the business of issuing tax invoices which would quickly slow shops down to a crawl. There are no less than 12 different retail schemes to choose from, each with a different calculation to determine the output tax from the takings.

As a retailer there are two hurdles you have to cross: choosing the retail scheme which suits you best, and operating that scheme correctly at the end of each tax period.

The first step is to get hold of Notice 727 'Retail schemes' which sets out the detailed rules for retailers, and pamphlet 727/6 'Choosing your retail scheme'. The pamphlet contains a handy flow chart designed to help you through the maze of rules and regulations about which scheme you can and cannot use. (You will have probably noticed by now from other publications that Customs and

Excise love flow charts, and they fondly imagine the public loves them too.) Each retail scheme has its own pamphlet in blue, green and white, from 727/7 (scheme A) through to 727/15 (scheme J).

Definition of a Retailer

The first rule of retail schemes is that only retailers can use them. Other service industries have to stick with the normal tax point rules set out in Chapter 2: Sales and Services. Customs and Excise define retailers by trade classification. When you register for VAT you have to choose your trade classification from Form VAT 41 which is sent to you along with the registration literature and Form VAT 1. If you choose your trade classification from group 24 'Retail distribution' then you are a retailer. If you have any other trade class then you are not a retailer, with the possible exception of group 28 'Miscellaneous Services'. If you have a different trade class and still think you are a retailer you should try writing to your local VAT office to state your case.

You might well find yourself in the situation where you have two different sides to your business, for example you might run a hardware shop with a joinery business as a sideline. In a case like this you would have to use the normal tax point rules for the joinery business but you could use a retail scheme for the hardware shop.

Another situation which might arise is that the hardware shop in this example might have a contract to supply other VAT registered businesses with goods from the shop, for example materials to a builder. Supplies like these which are separate from the shop itself have to be dealt with under the normal tax point and invoicing rules.

Another point to bear in mind is that retail schemes are only for taxable supplies. They are not for exempt supplies, so under no circumstances should you include money from things like the rent of the flat above your shop in your takings figure. The retail schemes themselves are merely different ways of working out how much of your takings is from the sale of standard-rated items and how much is from the sale of zero-rated items.

The Daily Gross Take (DGT)

The **daily gross take** is a very important figure because it is the central figure in all the retail schemes as well as being the total sales figure for each day's trading. Every day you are open for business you have to keep a record of this total so that you can work out your total takings for the tax period. Note that it is the gross figure which is required and not any other figure. The gross amount is obviously affected by several different factors.

Payments In and Out

Remember that the daily gross take is the total amount you have sold on a given day, whether standard or zero-rated. So, if you only open your till or draw to put money in then you should have few problems in working out your daily gross take. But should you take cash from the till to pay the window cleaner or the milkman, for example, you must keep a note of it, preferably in the till or draw, so that at the end of the day you can add it back in again. This is because the money in the till is still money you have received for selling goods on which output tax may have to be paid.

Again, if you pay the window cleaner or milkman with goods from your shop, you must add the selling price of these goods to your daily gross take because you have made a taxable supply and Customs and Excise want any output tax due on the full value of that supply. This works the same way with anything you take for yourself from your shop but this time you only have to add the cost price (including VAT) to your daily gross take figure. If, on the other hand, a customer returns goods you have sold and you give a refund then you can subtract this from the daily gross take because you are back to where you were before the supply was made.

Theft is a little more complicated. If someone steals cash from your till then you still have to include however much was stolen in your daily gross take. This sounds unfair but the principle is that a supply has been made and tax is therefore due. If, on the other hand, someone steals goods from your shop, then no adjustment need be made because no supply has taken place.

How to Work Out Your Daily Gross Take

There are two methods of doing this:

(1) The standard method
This is based on payments received for whatever you sell, be it standard or zero-rated. If you sell goods on credit, then you include the sales only as and when you are paid in your daily gross take.

(2) The optional method
This is based on what you charge rather than what you receive so if you sell on credit you should include the amount charged in your

daily gross take before you are actually paid. This is in addition to your normal takings figure at the end of the day.

Naturally the standard method is recommended, for who wants to account for output tax before being paid? It means you only have to think in terms of actual money.

How you record your daily gross takings figure is up to you. There are some very sophisticated tills on the market which, provided they are worked properly, are useful tools for the shopkeeper. If you do use a till and it produces readouts at the push of a button you will have to keep these for a full six years (see Chapter 7). Electronic tills produce two types of readout, the 'X' and the 'Z'. The 'X' is the readout you take without clearing the till back to nought, and is useful if you keep a check on different staff shifts or on a morning or afternoon's trading. The 'Z' on the other hand is the final cashing up readout and records the day's events as seen by the till. This is the part you will have to keep to show a visiting officer, because the final total, allowing for mistakes, should correspond to the daily gross take figure.

Deposits, Book Tokens and Vouchers

If you receive an advance payment for something you sell then this counts as a payment for a supply you have made so you have to include it in your daily gross take. But if, say, you lend or hire something to somebody and you take a deposit in case the something never comes back then this is not part of your daily gross take because no supply has been made. This is still the case even if the item is not returned.

As far as tokens and vouchers are concerned you will remember from Chapter 1 the principle that output tax is due on the full, or open market value, of a supply. So any book tokens, record tokens or special offer vouchers you accept in part or full payment for anything you sell count as real money when you come to count up your daily gross take. If you sell book or record tokens you only have to account for output tax if you sell them for more than the face value and then only on the difference between the two. Otherwise you can leave them out of your daily gross takings figure.

The Retail Schemes

Remember, the whole point of the different retail schemes is to split the standard and zero-rated sales so that you can calculate how much output tax is due each tax period. Whichever retail scheme you eventually choose and operate, you should stick to the calculation like a limpet. Do not try your own variation even if you think it is better as it may well rebound on you. Some schemes are more accurate than others, and these generally require more work. Choosing a retail scheme is up to you – use any you like as long as you meet the conditions laid down. Some you will instantly want to ignore and others you may not be able to use, so in the end you may find you only have a limited choice anyway.

The retail schemes themselves can be divided into three groups:

1 Establishing the liability at the point of sale (schemes A and F).
2 **Apportionment.** This is where you calculate the percentage of standard-rated goods sold and apply this to your daily gross take (schemes D, G, H and J).
3 **Mark-up.** This is where you apply your mark-up or a fixed mark-up to either standard or zero-rated goods you sell and work out the subsequent split of your daily gross take (schemes B, B1, B2, C, E and E1). Note that Customs and Excise talk about the mark-up and *not* the margin. The margin is profit related to sales whereas the mark-up is the profit related to purchases.

$$\text{Mark-up} = \frac{\text{profit}}{\text{cost}} \times 100$$

Scheme A – Pamphlet 727/7 'How to Work Scheme A'

Conditions

Scheme A is the only scheme you can use if all you sell are standard-rated goods and/or services. It is also the easiest to operate because there are no zero-rated sales to confuse matters.

Calculation

$$\text{Daily gross takings for the tax period} \times \text{VAT fraction} \left(\frac{7}{47}\right) = \text{output tax due}$$

Change in Tax Rate and/or Liability

If the tax rate changes simply do the calculation twice, once for the period up to the change and once at the end of the tax period. Add up the two figures to get the total output tax for the period. If the liability changes and something you sell becomes zero-rated you will have to change schemes.

Scheme F – Pamphlet 727/12 'How to Work Scheme F'

Conditions

If you can split your standard-rated and zero-rated sales *accurately* at the point when money changes hands, then this could be the scheme for you. You can do this however you like, using different tins, cash draws or an electronic till with enough buttons to record the type of sale being made. You have to be able to distinguish between standard-rated and zero-rated goods when you are adding up the totals at the time of the sale. Most people use different coloured price tags.

Calculation

$$\text{Standard rated daily gross takings} \times \text{VAT fraction} \left(\frac{7}{47}\right) = \text{output tax due}$$

Points to Watch

Because you are recording standard-rated and zero-rated sales separately this is one of the easiest schemes to operate. It is also the easiest to get wrong. Before you even think of operating this scheme you must be 100% sure that you can split the standard-rated and zero-rated sales with pinpoint accuracy. You may think this quite possible but suppose your assistant is operating the till and the shop is very busy. Can you be absolutely sure he or she is hitting the right button every single time? If you do decide to use scheme F it is a very good idea to check your output tax figure against another scheme (you could do a scheme D calculation, for example), just to make sure you are not making too many mistakes using scheme F. There should be only minor differences between the two different scheme results.

Change in Tax Rate and/or Liability

As with scheme A, if the tax rate changes simply calculate the output tax due up to the end of the old tax rate and calculate again at the end of the tax period using the new rate. The two figures together will give you your output tax for the period. If the liability changes remember to charge the correct rate of VAT on the goods affected and to change any identification system you may use.

Scheme D – Pamphlet 727/10 'How to Work Scheme D'

Conditions

Scheme D is based on working out the percentage of your sales which are standard-rated and requires an annual adjustment calculation. The conditions are:

1 That your taxable turnover is less than £500,000 per year. Remember your taxable turnover includes both standard-rated and zero-rated sales.
2 That if you supply services, or if you make or grow anything for sale, you have to account for the output tax on these separately.

If this will cause problems then you are probably better off with another scheme. This scheme is designed for the smaller shop such as the licensed grocer, where it works very well.

Calculation

There are two calculations to be done with scheme D, one at the end of each tax period and the other at the end of each tax year. For the calculations you have to keep a record of your standard-rated purchases which you buy in to sell on, as well as the total of all your purchases for sale in your shop in each tax period. At the end of each tax period the calculation for that period's purchases is:

$$\frac{\text{Total purchase price (including VAT) of standard-rated goods for onward sale}}{\text{Total purchase price (including VAT) of standard-rated } \textit{and} \text{ zero-rated goods for onward sale}} \times \text{Daily gross takings} \times \text{VAT fraction} \left(\frac{7}{47}\right) = \text{output tax due}$$

At the end of the tax year the calculation has to be done all over again, but this time using the whole year's figures. This is to take into account any abnormal periods when perhaps a lot of stock was brought in. The tax year runs to either 31 March, 30 April or 31 May, depending on when your VAT returns end (for monthly VAT returns it is 31 March).

The annual adjustment calculation is:

$$\frac{\text{Total purchase price (including VAT) of standard-rated goods bought for resale in year}}{\text{Total purchase price of standard-rated } \textit{and} \text{ zero-rated purchases bought for resale in year}} \times \text{Daily gross takings for year} \times \text{VAT fraction} \left(\frac{7}{47}\right) = \text{output tax due for year}$$

You then compare this figure with what you have already declared in output tax for the year. If it is more then you pay Customs and Excise the difference, and if it is less than you reclaim the difference. The amount of the adjustment is never very great but you should always remember to do it – after all, it might be money due to you. And if you forget to do it you can be sure that the visiting officer will do it for you.

Points to Watch

Because this scheme is based on purchase prices and not selling prices it is not very accurate if your standard-rated mark-up and your zero-rated mark-up vary a great deal. The effect of a higher zero-rated mark-up is to inflate the output tax you will end up paying so if this applies to you, you may well be better off with another scheme.

Change in Tax Rate and/or Liability

If the tax rate changes you have to close off your books and treat the time up to the change as a year, so you have to do the annual adjustment. However, if the tax rate changes within the next tax period after your last annual adjustment you can leave the annual adjustment until the year end is up. If the liability of anything you sell changes it is simply a case of remembering to swap round goods within the calculation.

Scheme G – Pamphlet 727/13 'How to Work Scheme G'

Conditions

Scheme G is very similar to scheme D. In fact if you like scheme D but exceed the turnover limit then this is the scheme you can move on to. You have to be able to work out your opening stock, or stock on hand in order to use the scheme. As with scheme D you cannot use the scheme for services, any home-made or home-grown supplies or catering supplies. If you still want to use the scheme and you provide any of these you have to account for the output tax separately.

Calculation

Because of the stock factor this scheme is split into two parts. The first calculation is for the first three tax periods, while the second is for all remaining tax periods. Before starting the scheme you have to carry out two stock-takes, one for the cost value (including VAT) of standard-rated goods, and one for the cost value (including VAT) of standard-rated *and* zero-rated goods. Both stock-takes are only for goods which are for onward sale in your shop(s).

The first calculation is for the first three periods you use the scheme:

$$\frac{\text{Total purchase price (incl. VAT) of standard-rated goods for onward sale since the scheme start + standard-rated stock figure (see above)}}{\text{Total purchase price (incl. VAT) of standard-rated } and \text{ zero-rated goods for onward sale bought since the scheme start + total stock figure (see above)}} \times \text{Daily gross takings} \times \text{VAT fraction}\left(\frac{7}{47}\right) \times \frac{9}{8} = \text{output tax due}$$

The $\frac{9}{8}$ at the end has the effect of adding ⅛ to your output tax. This is because Customs and Excise assume that because you are a larger business you will have varying mark-ups and this is to compensate for those to bring the scheme alongside the other more accurate schemes.

When you come to the fourth tax period you use a slightly different calculation:

$$\frac{\text{Total purchase price (incl. VAT) of standard-rated goods bought for onward sale in this tax period } and \text{ the last } three \text{ tax periods}}{\text{Total purchase price (incl. VAT) of standard-rated } and \text{ zero-rated goods for onward sale in this tax period } and \text{ the last } three \text{ tax periods}} \times \text{Daily gross takings (this period only)} \times \text{VAT fraction}\left(\frac{7}{47}\right) \times \frac{9}{8} = \text{output tax due}$$

This is the calculation for all later periods as well. Although it looks complicated, once you are used to what is going on it should present few problems.

Points to Watch

As with scheme D, because this scheme is based on purchase prices rather than selling prices you should consider the effect your different mark-ups have on the amount of output tax you will end up paying. If your zero-rated mark-ups are higher than your standard-rated ones then your output tax will be inflated, the more so because of the fact that you have to add on one eighth at the end.

Change in Tax Rate and/or Liability

If the tax rate changes you have to complete the period's calculation in two parts, one calculation at the time of the change and the other at the end of the tax period. The two totals together will give you your output tax. If the liability changes and it affects less than 5% of your taxable turnover per year you only have to change which goods go where in the calculation as appropriate. If more than 5% of your taxable turnover is affected you can:

1 Start operating the scheme from the very beginning again, or
2 Fight your way through the alternative in Notice 727. Not recommended.

Scheme B – Pamphlet 727/8 'How to Work Scheme B'

Conditions

Because this scheme is based on marking up your zero rated purchases to find their selling prices there are several conditions attached:

1 Your zero-rated sales have to be less than 50% of your total turnover. If they go over this figure, for example if there is a liability change, you will have to move onto another scheme.
2 Any services you supply must be standard-rated.
3 If you make catering supplies they have to be accounted for separately.

Calculation

The first thing to do is to isolate the zero-rated goods which you have bought, made or grown for onward sale in the tax period. Then work out how much you will sell them for, making allowances as necessary for wastage, special offers, etc. Having done that you can then do the calculation:

$$\left(\begin{array}{c}\text{Daily gross takings} - \text{selling price} \\ \text{of zero-rated goods}\end{array}\right) \times \text{VAT fraction} \left(\frac{7}{47}\right) = \text{output tax due}$$

Points to Watch

When you work out your zero-rated selling prices be careful not to include anything you buy from a trader who is not VAT registered in your zero-rated sales, unless you are sure that what you are buying *is* zero-rated. If you buy in a lot of zero-rated goods in one period you may find that you end up with a negative total for your output tax figure, and if this is the case simply write it on your VAT returns in brackets. This scheme works best when only a few zero-rated lines are being sold and the mark-up is easily calculated. Retail chemists have their own special version of this scheme (see Notice 727).

Change in Tax Rate and/or Liability

If the tax rate changes you have to close your books off and calculate as above for the period up to the change and also the period to the end of the tax period. The two figures together will give you your output tax for the period.

If the liability changes, apart from amending what goes where in your calculation, you also have to remember the 50% rule. If your zero-rated sales exceed 50% of your turnover you will have to change schemes. If the liability of services you provide changes so that standard-rated services become zero-rated you will have to leave them out of your scheme calculations.

Scheme B1 – Pamphlet 727/8A 'How to Work Scheme B1'

Conditions

These are similar to those imposed on scheme B because the two schemes are very alike, the difference being that scheme B1 has a stock adjustment which is done by means of an annual adjustment. The conditions are that:

1. You have to be able to work out the selling price of zero-rated goods held in stock at the beginning when you start to use the scheme and at the end of each year afterwards.
2. Any services you supply have to be standard-rated.
3. If you make catering supplies they have to be accounted for separately.

Note that there is *no* 50% turnover limit for scheme B1.

Calculation

As with scheme B you first have to work out the selling price of your zero-rated goods for onward sale (including goods bought in, made or grown), adjusting as necessary for wastage, special offers, etc. Before you start using the scheme you also have to work out, on a similar basis, the selling price of zero-rated goods held in stock. This figure is needed for the annual adjustment.

Having done all that at the end of each tax period the calculation is:

$$\left(\begin{array}{c}\text{Daily gross takings} - \text{selling price}\\ \text{of zero-rated goods}\end{array}\right) \times \text{VAT fraction} \left(\frac{7}{47}\right) = \text{output tax due}$$

When you come to the fourth tax period first do the calculation for that period as above. Then, before filling in the VAT return for the period, you have to do the annual adjustment:

$$\text{Daily gross takings} - \left(\begin{array}{c}\text{selling price of zero-rated goods}\\ \text{received in the last 4 tax periods +}\\ \text{zero-rated goods in stock at start of}\\ \text{year (see above)} - \text{selling price of}\\ \text{zero-rated goods in stock at the end}\\ \text{of the 4th tax period}\end{array}\right) \times \text{VAT fraction} \left(\frac{7}{47}\right) = \text{output tax due}$$

You then compare this figure with the output tax figures of your four VAT returns. If the difference is in your favour you reclaim this difference on your VAT return, but if the difference is in Customs and Excise's favour you pay them the difference.

Change in Tax Rate and/or Liability

If the tax rate changes you have to close off your books, do an annual adjustment and then start again. However, if the tax rate changes within the next tax period after your last annual adjustment you can leave the annual adjustment until the year end is up.

If the liability changes remember to swap goods round in the calculation. If any of your standard-rated services change to being zero-rated you will have to leave them out of your scheme calculations.

Scheme B2 – Pamphlet 727/8B 'How to Work Scheme B2'

Conditions

This scheme is a further variation on the theme of marking up zero-rated goods, but because the mark-ups are fixed by Customs and Excise there are certain conditions:

1 You cannot use the scheme if your taxable turnover is more than £500,000 per year. Remember your taxable turnover includes standard-rated *and* zero-rated goods.
2 Any services you supply have to be standard-rated.
3 You cannot use the scheme for home-made or home-grown zero-rated goods.
4 If you make catering supplies you have to account for them separately.

Calculation

First, the fixed mark-ups:

Food	20%
Books, maps etc	40%
Newspapers and magazines	33%
Children's clothes and footwear	35%
Other goods	15%

Then for each tax period you take the zero-rated goods bought in during that time and do the calculation:

$$\text{Daily gross takings} - \begin{array}{l}\text{Selling price of zero-rated goods}\\ \text{bought in during tax period and}\\ \text{marked up as above}\end{array} \times \begin{array}{l}\text{VAT}\\ \text{fraction}\end{array}\left(\frac{7}{47}\right) = \begin{array}{l}\text{output}\\ \text{tax due}\end{array}$$

Points to Watch

Obviously if your actual mark-ups are higher than those above then you will lose out on this scheme as you will pay more output tax than necessary. It works the other way too, so if your actual mark-ups are lower than these then you will pay less output tax than you would under another scheme. This is why there is a fairly low turnover limit for the scheme.

A quick way to do the actual mark-up with a calculator is to add 100% to the above mark-ups. The long way to do it is to take the purchase price, multiply by the fixed mark-up and then add this figure to the purchase price to get the marked-up selling price. So if you buy in food costing £100 the calculation is £100 × 20% = £20, £20 + £100 = £120 which is the marked-up selling price. The quick way is simply to calculate £100 × 120% = £120.

Change in Tax Rate and/or Liability

If the tax rate changes you have to carry out the period's calculation in two separate parts, one up to the change and one up to the end of the period. The two output tax totals added together will give you your period's output tax. If the liability changes remember to swap the affected goods around in the calculation.

Scheme C – Pamphlet 727/9 'How to Work Scheme C'

Conditions

This scheme also works on mark-ups, but the mark-up that you apply is determined by your trade class and is applied to your standard-rated goods for onward sale. Remember, your trade class is the group, or code number, that you chose from Form VAT 41 which best describes your business activity (see Chapter 1). Because of this there are quite a few conditions:

1 You have to have a trade class in the range 8201 to 8239. If you have forgotten yours you will find it on your certificate of registration.
2 Your taxable turnover has to be less than £90,000 per year. Remember, your taxable turnover is your standard *and* zero-rated sales.

3 You cannot use the scheme for services you supply.
4 You cannot use the scheme for home-made or home-grown goods.
5 If you make catering supplies you have to account for them separately.

Calculation
Firstly, the fixed mark-ups for each trade class:

trade class	description of business	mark-up to be used
8207	off-licences	15.5%
8214	confectioners, newsagents, tobacconists	15.5%
8201	grocers	20%
8202	dairymen	20%
8203	butchers	20%
8204	fishmongers	20%
8206	bakers	20%
8205	greengrocers and fruit sellers	40%
8222	radio & electrical shops (*not* radio or TV rental)	40%
8225	bicycle shops	40%
8227	chemist & photographic shops	40%
8215	footwear shops	60%
8218	fur shops	60%
8233	florists, nursery & garden shops	60%
8213	mail order businesses	70%
8229	jewellers	75%
no specific trade class	health & wholefood shops	50%
all other group 24 trade classes	N/A	50%

The calculation for each period is:

$$\text{Selling price (incl. VAT) of standard-rated goods after fixed mark-up applied} \times \text{VAT fraction} \left(\frac{7}{47}\right) = \text{output tax due}$$

Points to Watch

Because mark-ups are fixed this scheme is only really suitable if your actual mark-up is equal to, or more than, the fixed mark-ups above. If they are less you will pay too much output tax. But if they are more you will end up the winner, and this is why there is such a low turnover limit. Once your business grows and exceeds the limit you have to change to another scheme, but if it is only inflation which carries you over the limit you can continue with it. For a quick way to apply the mark-up have a look at the 'Points to Watch' section of the previous scheme, B2.

Change in Tax Rate and/or Liability

If the tax rate changes you have to calculate for the period in two parts, once for the period up to the change and once for the subsequent time up to the end of the tax period itself. The two figures added together will give you your output tax figure for the period. If the liability of anything you sell changes, simply remember to include it or exclude it from the calculation as appropriate.

Scheme E – Pamphlet 727/11 'How to Work Scheme E'

Conditions

Because scheme E is based on marking-up standard-rated goods for onward sale, with stock taken into account, there are several conditions:

1 You have to know what standard-rated stock you have when you start to use the scheme. Otherwise you can use the previous three months' purchases for resale – simply take their selling price.
2 You have to be able to work out the selling prices of standard-rated goods by line, as you cannot simply apply your overall mark-up to everything.
3 If you supply standard-rated services or catering you have to account for these separately.

Calculation

The first thing to do is to isolate the standard-rated goods in stock which you have bought, made or grown, and mark them up, line by line. For the first first tax period in which you use the scheme the calculation is:

$$\text{Selling price (incl. VAT) of goods in stock for onward sale + any bought, made or grown for resale in tax period} \times \text{VAT fraction} \left(\frac{7}{47}\right) = \text{output tax due}$$

For every other tax period after this, the calculation is simplified:

$$\text{Selling price (incl. VAT) of goods bought, made or grown for onward sale in tax period} \times \text{VAT fraction} \left(\frac{7}{47}\right) = \text{output tax due}$$

Points to Watch

Because you pay the output tax on goods not yet sold, you are best using this scheme if you have a fairly fast turnover. But if you stop using the scheme you can reclaim output tax paid on goods not yet sold, and simply adjust your VAT return accordingly.

Change in Tax Rate and/or Liability

If the tax rate changes simply treat that tax period as being in two parts and work out the calculation twice, once up to the change and once to the period end. The two figures added together will give you the output tax for that period. If the liability of anything you sell changes simply swap it in or out of the calculation as necessary.

Scheme E1 – Pamphlet 727/11A 'How to Work Scheme E1'

Conditions

1 You have to keep very detailed stock records. This is because for each tax period you need a standard-rated opening stock figure and a standard-rated closing stock figure (which then becomes your opening stock figure for the next period).

This stock figure is needed for each line of standard-rated goods you sell.

2 If you supply standard-rated services or catering you have to account for these separately.

Calculation

This has to be done for each line of standard-rated goods you sell, be they bought, made or grown for onward sale:

$$\left(\begin{array}{l}\text{Number of items}\\\text{in a particular}\\\text{standard-rated}\\\text{line in stock at}\\\text{start of period}\end{array} + \begin{array}{l}\text{Number of items}\\\text{in same line}\\\text{brought in for}\\\text{onward sale}\\\text{during tax period}\end{array} - \begin{array}{l}\text{Number of items}\\\text{in same line in}\\\text{stock at the end}\\\text{of the tax}\\\text{period}\end{array}\right) \times \begin{array}{l}\text{Selling}\\\text{price}\\\text{(incl.}\\\text{VAT) of}\\\text{the item}\end{array}$$

$$\times \text{VAT fraction} \left(\frac{7}{47}\right) = \text{output tax due for the line}$$

So obviously you will have to repeat the calculation for each line of goods which, added together, will give you the final output tax figure for all your standard-rated goods for onward sale.

Points to Watch
If you like paperwork this is the scheme for you, but you will be compensated in the knowledge that it is possibly the most accurate scheme there is. It is perhaps best used by businesses with low stocks of standard-rated goods because the stock checks are less of a problem. And there is more time to think about all the paper you will need.

Change in Tax Rate and/or Liability
Again, if the tax rate changes, you will have to treat the period up to the change and the period to the end of the tax period proper as two different periods. The results of the two calculations added together will give you your output tax for that tax period. Unfortunately, if the liability changes you have to follow the same procedure and calculate the tax period in two separate parts.

Scheme H – Pamphlet 727/14 'How to Work Scheme H'

Conditions
Because this scheme uses apportionment, mark-ups and stock figures it is best suited to the larger businesses with computer-based operations. The conditions are:

1 You have to know what stock you have when starting to use the scheme.
2 You cannot use the scheme for supplies of catering.

Calculation
Because of the stock factor this scheme is split into two parts. The first part is for the first three tax periods, while the second is for the fourth and all remaining tax periods. Before starting to use the scheme you have to work out:

1 The selling price, including VAT, of standard-rated goods in stock for onward sale.
2 The selling price, including VAT, of standard-rated *and* zero-rated goods in stock for onward sale.

When working out your selling prices for the calculation be very careful to allow for wastage, theft, special offers and so on. This is because once you have set the prices you cannot go back and alter them.

For the first three periods in which you use the scheme the calculation is:

$$\frac{\text{Selling price (incl. VAT) of standard-rated goods for onward sale bought, made or grown since you started the scheme + standard-rated stock figure (see above)}}{\text{Selling price (incl. VAT) of standard } \textit{and} \text{ zero-rated goods for onward sale bought, made or grown since you started the scheme + your total standard and zero-rated stock figure (see above)}} \times \text{Daily gross takings} \times \text{VAT fraction} \left(\frac{7}{47}\right) = \text{output tax}$$

For the fourth and later tax periods the calculation changes slightly:

$$\frac{\text{Selling price (incl. VAT) of standard-rated goods for onward sale bought, made or grown in this tax period } \textit{and} \text{ the last } \textit{three} \text{ tax periods}}{\text{Selling price (incl. VAT) of standard-rated } \textit{and} \text{ zero-rated goods for onward sale bought, made or grown in this tax period } \textit{and} \text{ the last } \textit{three} \text{ tax periods}} \times \text{Daily gross takings} \times \text{VAT fraction} \left(\frac{7}{47}\right) = \text{output tax}$$

Points to Watch

The only thing to watch here is that you operate the scheme correctly and that your selling prices are as accurate as possible.

Change in Tax Rate and/or Liability

If the tax rate changes you have to work through that period's calculation in two parts, one for the time up to the change, and one for the time to the end of the tax period. The two figures added together will give you the total output tax for the period. If the liability of any of your supplies changes and it affects no more than 5% of your taxable turnover per year you only need to change the liability of the goods you buy in as appropriate. More than this and you can either:

1 Start operating the scheme from the very beginning again, or
2 Fight your way through the alternative in Notice 727. Not recommended.

Scheme J – Pamphlet 727/15 'How to Work Scheme J'

Conditions

This is the final scheme and Customs and Excise's *pièce de résistance*. It combines virtually every feature from every scheme in an orgy of stocktaking and calculation. You will need a very detailed stock control system for this scheme, and it really requires a computer-based till operation. Apart from this the conditions are:

1 You cannot use the scheme for services.
2 Any supplies of catering have to be accounted for separately.

Calculation

This involves a calculation for each tax period and an annual adjustment which you make before you come to do your fourth VAT return. But before you start to use the scheme you have to work out:

1 The selling price, including VAT, of standard-rated goods in stock for onward sale.
2 The selling price, including VAT, of standard *and* zero-rated goods in stock for onward sale.

As with scheme H you have to be as accurate as possible when working out your selling prices and allow for theft, wastage, special offers and so on. This is because once you have decided on your selling prices you cannot change them. You also have to mark them up by line rather than apply an average mark-up.

For each tax period the calculation is as follows:

$$\frac{\text{Selling price (incl. VAT) of standard-rated goods for onward sale bought, made or grown since the start of the year + standard-rated stock figure (see above)}}{\text{Selling price (incl. VAT) of standard } \textit{and} \text{ zero-rated goods for onward sale bought, made or grown since the start of the year + your total standard and zero-rated stock figure (see above)}} \times \text{Daily gross takings for period} \times \text{VAT fraction}\left(\frac{7}{47}\right) = \text{output tax for period}$$

Note that you have to include goods received since the start of the year. The year starts with the first day of the first tax period in which you first use the scheme.

When you come to the fourth period after beginning the scheme you still have to do the calculation as above. But before you fill in your VAT return you have to do the annual adjustment as follows:

$$\frac{\text{Standard-rated stock figure (see above) + selling price (incl. VAT) of standard-rated goods for onward sale in stock over last 4 tax periods - Selling price (incl. VAT) of standard-rated goods in stock at year end}}{\text{Total standard and zero-rated stock figure (see above) + selling price VAT) of standard \textit{and} zero-rated goods for onward sale in stock over last 4 tax periods - Selling price (incl. VAT) of standard \textit{and} zero-rated goods in stock at year end}} \times \text{Daily gross takings for last 4 periods} \times \text{VAT fraction} \left(\frac{7}{47}\right) = \text{output tax for year}$$

You then look at the output tax you have declared for the same periods, and if the difference is in your favour you reclaim the difference. If it is in Customs and Excise's favour you pay them the difference.

Points to Watch
Although it is a very complicated scheme it is also a very accurate scheme. There are two adaptations you can use but you have to convince your local VAT office that you are losing out under the normal calculation because of your particular stock movements.

Change in Tax Rate and/or Liability
If the tax rate changes you have to treat the period up to the change as a complete year and do the annual adjustment. You also have to do another calculation at the end of the tax period to find out the output tax figure for that period. The two figures added together will give you your total output tax for the entire period.

If the liability changes and it affects not more than 5% of your taxable turnover per year you only have to change the liability of the goods for onward sale within the calculation as appropriate. More than this and you have to follow the same procedure as for a change in the tax rate (see above).

Choosing a Retail Scheme

Having looked through the different schemes you may still be wondering which one to choose. It is entirely up to you. The only requirement is that you meet all the conditions of your chosen scheme. This fact will probably prevent you from using most of the schemes, thus making your choice that much easier.

The best way to approach the problem is first to go through them all and make a note of all the ones you can use. Then you can make your choice. Your accountant should be able to help you choose but he or she may have a particular favourite and this might not be your first choice. You could always try operating the different calculations on an invented set of figures just to see if you can spot any likely problem areas cropping up.

You can, if you so desire, mix schemes but this inevitably causes complications. Some schemes cannot merge together, turnover limits still apply, and you still have the added complication of operating two schemes. If you want to use a particular scheme and cannot use it for all your supplies, for example if you use a mark-up scheme and supply catering services, then simply account for these separately.

Changing Schemes

This can only be done, generally speaking, after a full year using the scheme you want to abandon. Do not forget to do the annual adjustment if you are using schemes D, B1 and J. Of course there may be other times when you have to change schemes mid-year: for example if you use an electronic till to operate scheme F and it breaks down after three months in which case you will have to find some other way to account for the VAT due. If this happens to you, you should write to your local VAT office asking for guidance on your particular circumstances. If you change schemes without permission then a visiting officer may well work out the tax due on the scheme you abandoned, and if it is more than you subsequently paid, issue an assessment for the difference.

Retail Exports

As a retailer you can, if you want to, operate the **retail export** scheme so that your overseas customers can get back any VAT they had to pay on standard-rated goods you sold them. You will probably be aware of the scheme anyway because tourist shops tend to advertise the scheme in their windows. The term 'retail export' is misleading because exports are zero-rated. With this scheme you still charge VAT but you can refund it once you have received proof that the customer has left the country, and is indeed a foreign resident.

If you are considering this scheme you will need Notice 704

'Retail exports'. If you go on to operate the scheme you should get hold of as many copies of the VAT 407 'Retail export scheme form' and pamphlet 704/1 'VAT refunds for visitors to the United Kingdom' as possible from your local VAT office.

What You Can Sell

You can use the scheme to sell most standard-rated goods. The only exceptions are:

(1) Motor vehicles
There is a special scheme for these outlined in Notice 705 'Personal exports: new motor vehicles' and Notice 703 'Exports'.

(2) Boats
Again there is a special scheme, leaflet 703/2 'Sailaway boats supplied for export'.

(3) Exports to be used in business
These are dealt with in Chapter 6: Imports and Exports.

Apart from these exceptions, what you sell under the scheme is very much up to you. You can, if you wish, sell only certain items or set a limit, for example only goods costing more than £200, for goods you sell under the scheme. You can also charge an administrative fee to cover your time and incidental expenses like postage.

If the VAT is not very great the chances are that the customer will end up paying the same, or even more, in administration costs and time than he or she would have done if the VAT had simply been paid. But it helps business along.

To Whom You Can Sell

You can only use the scheme to sell goods to overseas visitors. The conditions are:

1 That your customer has not been living here for more than one year in the last two years
2 That your customer leaves the UK within three months of purchasing the goods.

If your customer lives in another European country different rules apply, and there are monetary limits. To use the scheme an EC traveller has to buy goods worth more than the following limits:

1 £58 if your customer is going to live, or already lives, in Eire.

2 £210 if your customer is going to live, or already lives, in Greece.
3 £230 if your customer is going to live, or already lives, in Denmark.
4 £265 if your customer is going to live, or already lives, in any other EC country.

As well as these limits applying, the customer from the EC has to declare the goods to Customs on arrival in his or her own country rather than when leaving the UK. However, when the single market finally arrives the chances are that the scheme will no longer apply to EC citizens as they will be treated just like the rest of Britain.

How to Operate the Scheme

If you do decide to operate the scheme remember that as the retailer, you are the key person in the whole affair. You are the one who decides to adopt the scheme, you decide on any conditions and set any extra charges for administrative expenses, and you are the one who sends the refund back to the customer. At this stage it is worth mentioning that if you do make a charge for your administrative expenses then that charge is a zero-rated supply.

There are three stages in the process of operating the scheme:

1 When you actually sell the goods

The first thing to do here is to have a look at the customer's passport or identity papers to make sure that he or she does indeed live overseas. Also have a look at the return ticket to make sure that the customer will be leaving the country within the 3-month time limit.

(*a*) *Fill in Form VAT 407*. You can, if you wish, use a proper tax invoice instead (see Chapter 2) but the VAT 407 is much better because it is tailor-made for the scheme and there should be no quibbles from Customs and Excise. Do not forget to fill it all in, and in as much detail as possible. This is because when your customer actually leaves the country the Customs Officer will want to be satisfied that the goods he or she sees are the same as the ones on the form.

(*b*) *Give the customer a stamped addressed envelope to post the form back to you.*

(*c*) *Enter the sale as normal and charge VAT.*

2 When the customer actually leaves the country

He or she will get Form VAT 407 stamped by Customs on leaving the country. It is worth noting here that Customs *must* see the goods before stamping the form. So make sure your customer realises that if the article cannot travel as hand baggage he or she will have to leave enough time before departure to fish it out of the suitcase to show to Customs.

If your customer fails this hurdle and does not get hold of the required stamp there are one or two acceptable alternatives. A freight forwarding shipment invoice, a local tax receipt or an export document signed and stamped by a local official are all acceptable as other evidence.

3 When you receive proof of export

This is when you send back the VAT your customer has paid. If it is in a different tax period to when you sold the goods, you should still account for the VAT in your return until you receive proof of export. Only then can you refund the money and zero-rate the sale. How you refund the money is up to you and your customer to decide. You may wish to discuss this side of it with your bank before you start to use the scheme.

6

Imports and Exports

Introduction · Imports · Exports · International Services · The Single European Market

Introduction

As a business you will find it quite hard to avoid becoming involved in importing and exporting, even if only for the odd transaction here and there. Imported goods are as much a part of the fabric of British life as the car in the driveway (itself often a foreign product). Even if you cannot at present see any situation where you might get involved, the chances are that one day you will be looking for new markets abroad or find a foreign product to fill a gap in your range.

This is especially so in a fluctuating economic climate. The gloomier the economy looks at home the more you will want to sell to better off countries abroad. And in boom times at home there is always increased demand for foreign goods. The creation of the Single European Market is of course another major reason to persuade British business to look beyond the home market.

As far as VAT goes, the basic position is quite simple. You pay VAT on imports but you can zero-rate exports. (The situation as regards services is a little more complicated – more on this later.) The notices you should obtain copies of are:

- Notice 702 'Imports and warehoused goods'
- Notice 703 'Exports'
- Notice 741 'International Services'

Imports

Everyone who imports goods is charged VAT where applicable. As a VAT registered person you will be able to reclaim this VAT, but remember the rules about claiming input tax. So if you import, say, outdoor jackets from the USA and decide to order a few extra for all the family, remember these are not for your business and you cannot reclaim the VAT.

Curiously, the amount of VAT charged on your import is calculated *after* all the other customs (and excise) duties have been applied. These vary according to what is being imported but if you want to find out the rate for your own particular goods you should ring up your local Customs and Excise office. Note that this is not always the same as your local VAT office.

Imports can be split into three types: direct imports, postal imports and imports from bond, each with their own procedure and paperwork.

Direct Imports

This is the normal import procedure, whereby you simply buy the goods from abroad and, at the time of importation, pay the duties and VAT. If you only do this once in a blue moon then you might want to handle it all yourself, for example if you bring in some goods from a holiday or business trip. In this case you could clear the goods as you come through Customs, providing you have the money.

If, on the other hand, you import regularly or even occasionally you would be well advised to use an agent. There are clusters of agents around every port and airport in the country so finding one should not be a problem. They are full-time professionals whose whole lives are geared to clearing goods through the system. Using one of them will make life much more tolerable for you.

Deferred Accounting

If you are a regular importer you can use this system to pay any VAT and duties due on your imports. As you import something, instead of having to pay the VAT up front, Customs and Excise remove it from your bank account by direct debit on the 15th day of the next month. However you do have to arrange for a bank or insurance company to act as a guarantor for your use of the system (Customs and Excise are not fools!). You can still use your agent to do all the donkey work and pay by deferring the VAT and duties.

The notice to get hold of is Notice 101 'Deferring duty, VAT, and other charges'. It is not a VAT publication but a Customs one so you will need to contact your nearest Customs and Excise office to get hold of a copy.

Evidence Required
Before you can reclaim any VAT you have paid on imported goods you must have the correct evidence in your possession. This comes in the shape of an A4 sheet of paper imaginatively called a C79. This is produced by the Customs and Excise computer once a month and sent to your registered address, the address you put on your VAT 1 when you registered as your principal place of business.

If you register for VAT and immediately start importing, you may find problems here because there is a time lapse before your details go onto the computer. If this happens the only thing you can do is ring up your VAT office and ask them to sort you out. Do remember that you can only reclaim input tax once you have this document. If you try to reclaim input tax too early without it you could well incur interest and a penalty (see Chapter 1).

Imports from Bond

Goods which are placed in bonded warehouses are treated like exports so they can be zero-rated. Once in the warehouse the goods stay free of VAT as long as they remain in bond. So a whisky or liqueur company which leaves barrels full of hard liquor in bond over the years only has to pay VAT if and when they are brought out of bond and into the home market. Even if the goods are bought and sold many times whilst there they continue to be VAT-free as long as they remain in the bonded warehouse. It is only the person who imports them from bond who has to go through the import procedure. It is worth noting that only goods which carry duty can be placed in a bonded warehouse, you cannot send something there which only carries VAT.

Evidence Required
If you take goods out of a bonded warehouse you have to pay the VAT and duties. The evidence required is still form C79, so do not forget to wait for it to arrive before reclaiming the VAT. As with direct imports you can use the deferred accounting system to pay Customs and Excise.

Postal Imports

The procedure here is somewhat different. There are three types of postal import:

1 For goods worth up to and including £2000 but which are not delivered by datapost

There should be a customs declaration with the parcel showing your VAT registration number as well as a detailed description of the contents. You then account for any VAT due as output tax on your VAT return. Whether you can then reclaim it all back as input tax is subject to the normal rules covering the deduction of input tax (see Chapters 3 and 4). This sounds as if it might be complicated but really all you are doing is charging yourself output tax because no-one else is. This is called **postponed accounting**. You should always follow the process of declaring the VAT as output tax in box 1 of your return and reclaiming it in box 2.

2 For goods worth up to and including £2000 and delivered by datapost

This is much more simple. The Post Office will collect the VAT from you when they deliver the parcel. The charge docket on the parcel then becomes the evidence needed to reclaim the VAT. This is the only system you can use for goods of this value and delivered in this way.

3 For goods worth more than £2000

For these Customs and Excise will send you a declaration to fill in which you have to return with the invoice showing how much the goods are worth. If you use the deferred accounting system you can pay as normal but everyone else has to pay up straight away. The evidence you need in order to reclaim the input tax is copy 8 of a piece of paper called the Single Administrative Document (SAD). Customs and Excise will send this to you once you have paid all the VAT and any duty, etc.

Exports

Exports are zero-rated. But to be an export the goods have to be sent out of the UK, so delivering them to an address in this country does not count, even if they are merely going there as part of their journey overseas. The only exception to this is if you use an agent, for example an export house (more on this later). If you send goods to the Isle of Man you are *not* exporting but if you trade with the Channel Islands then your sales *are* exports as far as VAT goes. Apart from these exceptions the UK includes waters inside the 3-mile limit so supplies to oil rigs outside these waters count as exports.

To be able to zero-rate an export you must have evidence of export, otherwise a visiting VAT officer will assume that it was a normal UK sale and send you a bill for the output tax you should have accounted for.

The evidence you need depends on how you send the goods abroad. You should also keep all those other bits of paper such as correspondence, invoices and payment details, just in case they are called for.

By Sea or Air

The best evidence to get hold of here is the shipped bill of lading, the sea waybill, the air waybill or a certificate of shipment. These all show that the goods actually went somewhere. The bill of lading itself, although generally acceptable, only indicates that the goods were received for later transport. If all you have is one of these you should be prepared, if you are asked, to get hold of evidence showing that the goods left the country. The same evidence is required if you export by lorry which carries the goods all the way to their destination.

By Freight Forwarder

If you use a freight forwarder to export smaller items then your export will probably be combined with many others. You can still zero-rate your export even though the goods are going in the first instance to the freight forwarder, but you have to have either a copy of the ship or air documents (as above), or a certificate of shipment from the freight forwarder. This has to show on which ship or aircraft your goods were transported and through which port or airport, the date the goods went, the container number and a full description of the goods exported. This is called a groupage or consolidation transaction.

By Post

The evidence of export here is the Post Office certificate of posting. Do not forget you will also need to fill in a customs declaration. If the goods you are sending are worth more than £100 you also have to attach Form VAT 444 which you get from your local VAT office, *not* from the Post office.

By Export House and Export Packer

Export houses are businesses which arrange and sometimes put up the money for exports. If you are contacted by an export house to send some goods overseas the liability of your supply depends on who you are supplying to. If the goods are delivered straight to a port or airport, or to an independent export packer for immediate export, then the liability is zero-rated. But you will still need the normal evidence for shipment by sea or air to prove that the goods have indeed been exported. If this proves difficult you can use a certificate of shipment from the export packer like that issued by freight forwarders (see above). If, on the other hand, you deliver to the export house itself then your supply is to the export house, so you will have to charge and account for output tax in the normal way.

Exports and Output Tax

The problem with exports is that in order to zero-rate your supply, you have to have evidence of export. So, if at the end of your tax period you have zero-rated an export but have not yet got the evidence required, you should account for output tax as if it had not been exported. This is a precaution against interest and penalty because you might, for some unforeseen reason, never obtain the evidence. Of course if the required evidence turns up in the next tax period you can simply reclaim the output tax you originally paid. At the end of each and every tax period you should have the necessary evidence for each and every export you have made.

Temporary Exports

If you send goods out of the country with the intention of having them back again, for example if you take part in trade fairs or exhibitions, you should make sure you tell Customs what is going on so that you do not have to waste time on the import/export procedure. The relevant notice is Notice 236 'Returned goods: free of duty and tax'.

International Services

There is a different procedure again with the import or export of services. If you are involved, or plan to be involved in either of these you need to get hold of Notice 741 'International Services'.

Export of Services

To be able to zero-rate your services you have to be able to show that whoever is receiving them is outside the UK (including the 3-mile limit). There are no special documents needed as evidence but you will be expected to be able to show from the invoice, contract, letters, etc. that your supply is going outside the UK. This could be a problem for services supplied to oil rigs outside the 3-mile limit where, for example, as a diver your contract might be with the UK office. In this case do make sure you have something to prove that your work is being carried out beyond the 3-mile limit. In cases of doubt simply charge VAT as normal.

Importing Services – The Reverse Charge

If an overseas business makes certain supplies of services to you as a VAT registered UK business then you have to charge yourself output tax on those supplies. This may sound a bit strange but the idea is to prevent foreign firms from undercutting British ones by getting away with not charging VAT. It is merely an extension of the rule that VAT is paid on imports, except that the business importing the services has to charge itself the VAT. The amount of this VAT that can then be reclaimed is then subject to the normal conditions (for example, partial exemption or non-business).

The services affected are known as Schedule 3 services because they are listed in schedule 3 to the VAT Act 1983:

- The transfer of a copyright, patent, licence or trade mark
- Advertising services
- Services provided by consultants. This includes people like engineers, lawyers, accountants, market researchers and translators. It does not include medical consultants
- Being paid *not* to do something
- Banking, finance and insurance services
- Supplying staff
- The hire of goods (not including transport)
- The procurement of any of the above services

If you receive any of these services from abroad you first have to convert the charge into pounds and pence. This then becomes the VAT-exclusive amount, so you have to multiply by the rate of VAT in force to find the output tax you have to charge yourself. Simply put this output tax together with all your other output tax in box 1 of the VAT return. If you are not partially exempt and the supply is wholly for your business you can reclaim it all back in box 2 with all your other input tax. This output tax you charge yourself is called the **reverse charge**.

If you do happen to be partially exempt (see Chapter 4) you will have to put the input tax into the appropriate part of the partial exemption calculation. If you are using a special method which is based on the value of your supplies you must not include the reverse charge supplies in the calculation.

If a UK company which is partially exempt, and therefore unable to reclaim all its input tax, decides to hire an accountant from overseas to try to get away with not paying VAT on his or her fees, then it would be disappointed. The company would still have to charge itself the VAT and would not be able to reclaim it all back as input tax. So it might as well have hired a UK firm anyway.

As with everything else, if you are in any doubt about how to account for the reverse charge then ask for advice. If you do not do the calculation then the visiting VAT officer will.

The Single European Market

VAT is the European tax. So the next time your VAT return comes through your letter-box, you can console yourself with the thought that all over this cradle of western civilisation, people are struggling, sweating and swearing as they try to work out what goes where. Sometimes Brussels stirs itself and issues commands so that everyone knows who is in charge, which is why we now have VAT on certain supplies of fuel and power.

The Single Market – Imports and Exports

In theory, the creation of a single market will mean that we are all one big happy trading bloc. Therefore sales to other EC countries will become normal commercial transactions with output tax charged in one country and reclaimed in another.

However, in reality, you might have to wait for a considerable time before this happens. In the meantime just carry on until

Customs and Excise says otherwise. If you are involved in imports and exports to other EC countries you can get a slick publication from Customs and Excise called 'The Single Market Report'. The address to write to is:

PO Box 1992
Dorset House
Stamford Street
London SE1 9LE

Apart from telling you what a splendid job Customs and Excise are doing on your behalf, it also gives you the latest on if and when the EC will ever get its collective act together.

The eventual idea is that what is called the 'origin' system (where you charge your EC customer output tax, who then recovers it as input tax), will take over from the present 'destination' system (where you zero-rate the export). However, this is unlikely to occur before the year 2000.

Part of the problem is that everybody is using different VAT rates. Ireland, for example, has a top rate of 25%, then three more at 10%, 5% and 2% as well as a zero rate. So the UK is quite well off with only a standard and a zero rate.

You will also be glad to know that the all-important business of collecting statistics has not been forgotten. At the moment these are collected on the Customs and Excise computer at the time of import and export but when this stops you, the trader, will be lumbered with the job.

7

Book-keeping and VAT

You, Your Books and Your Accountant · Computers · Correcting Errors and The VAT Account

You, Your Books and Your Accountant

Once you become VAT registered you have to shake off any casual methods and get down to some serious book-keeping. Have a look at the chapter in Notice 700 'The VAT Guide' on records and accounts, because this part of the guide is law. Basically everything you do as a VAT registered person has to be recorded and every piece of paper that records what you do has to be kept, all so that Customs and Excise can come along and check it. Make no mistake, everything means *everything*. It does not matter that some of your supplies may be zero-rated or exempt, because if you do it you have to record it.

Not only do you have to keep and maintain books, records and associated paperwork but it all has to be arranged so that it can be followed with as much ease as possible. So if you set up a system whose logic is known only to yourself, a visiting VAT officer will tell you to start all over again so that he or she can check what you have been doing.

Setting Up a System

Naturally you will want to consult your accountant about your method of book-keeping. After all, he or she will be doing your accounts for the bank, the Inland Revenue and Companies House (if you are a limited company).

When you are thinking about a system to use it is useful to go back to the very basics and think about what is being recorded. Basically you want to record money in and money out, income and expenditure, outputs and inputs. So the simpler you can keep things the better. For the smaller business this will mean a sales book and a purchase book of some description, or the two combined into one as in the Simplex books. For a small business on the Cash Accounting scheme or a retailer this should be adequate because output tax is paid only when the money is in your possession. And you can tie it all in nicely with the bank statements.

Normal Invoice Traders

For everyone else there are two factors to consider regarding VAT. Not only do you want to record the movement of money in and out of your business but you also need to record invoices by date so you can put the right ones in the right VAT returns. If you want to stick to a cash book system you should consider recording sales and purchase invoices separately, purely for VAT.

If, on the other hand, you want to keep sales and purchases together you could set up a sales and purchase day book type system, where invoices are entered as they are received but where there are separate columns for recording details of payments received. The purchase side does have the advantage in that it is up to you when you reclaim the input tax due to you, so you could keep a purchase book purely on a cash basis, if you wanted to.

Whatever books you decide to keep, remember that Customs and Excise will expect to be able to cross reference invoices to entries in the books, and vice versa. On the sales side, your book should include columns for:

Date	Invoice No.	Customer	Amount (ex. VAT)	VAT	VAT Incl. Amount

Apart from these basics you could have extra columns for zero-rated and exempt supplies, and the type of sale, i.e. whether it is a sale of assets or a straightforward business sale. At the end of the tax period it is then a simple exercise to complete your VAT return, especially if you keep running totals.

On the purchase side a similar system could be adopted. Again you split the type of purchase up into any one of a dozen or so columns, such as purchases for resale, running expenses, buying of assets, etc. When it comes to recording the invoice number do not try and record the invoice number already there but write one of your own instead on the invoice. Otherwise the supplier's invoice number will mean nothing to anybody. You may also like to keep a petty cash book for petrol, parking tickets and so on. If you do, do not forget to transfer the VAT to your VAT account at the end of the tax period.

Invoices

Naturally you should keep *all* your invoices. You have to keep copies of all your sales invoices as well as the original purchase ones (*note: photocopies will not do*). There are two ways you can file your sales and purchase invoices: either in date order as they appear in your books, or in alphabetical supplier order. Some people prefer one way, some the other. Whichever you choose you should still make sure that cross referencing can easily be carried out. A compromise which gives you the best of both worlds is to file the actual invoices in date order as they appear in your books, but to file supplier statements in alphabetical order. Technically input tax cannot be reclaimed on statements so the visiting officer will want to see the actual invoices and, if they are filed in date order, they will be much easier to check for both of you.

The 6-year Rule

You have to keep all your books for 6 years, so theoretically Customs and Excise could ring you up out of the blue and demand production of the whole lot going back the full 6 years, though it is unlikely they ever would. 'Books and records' covers everything: invoices, bank statements, till receipts, bank paying-in books, credit notes, contracts, annual accounts, import and export documents and so on. If it is on paper, microfilm or computer and it is to do with your business then you have to keep it for 6 years.

The only way you can avoid this rule is by writing to your local VAT office and asking for permission to get rid of some of your paperwork. If you have problems with storage, especially if you are a small business, this should not be too much of a problem.

You, Your Accountant and VAT

He or she is a very important figure in your business, and choosing one is a bit like finding a suitable doctor. Remember that accountancy is a pretty complex business, so do not be surprised if your accountant is not aware of the finer points of every direction, instruction or order issued by Customs and Excise. VAT, after all, is only a part of the financial complexities facing businesses today.

Some accountancy firms, especially the bigger national ones, have sections which deal in nothing but VAT. These are quite often staffed by ex-VAT officers, so if you do hire their services you are generally assured of technical competence. But it is a bit like going to Harley Street, in that you get brains at a price. This is not to say that the smaller firms are less competent, merely that you are not generally getting the services of a specialist.

It is worth pointing out that in an appeal against a penalty or surcharge on grounds of 'reasonable excuse' one of the two reasons *not* accepted is reliance on a third party. The other reason is not having any money (more on this in Chapter 9).

Computers

You may well be tempted by one of these. After all, anything which takes the pain out of book-keeping has to be good. However, do not imagine that all your VAT problems will be solved by installing a computer. Before buying one ask yourself what you want it to do. There are two ways you can use them.

1 Spreadsheet

This is where the computer merely does the same job as the books. It simply records everything you put into it in the same way as your books are laid out. Anything you want to do to those records you have to do yourself, as the computer merely stores all the information you wish to keep.

2 Accounting Packages

If you are going to use a computer this is the way to do it. Having bought a package, you can use the machine to do most of the donkey work for you. When you make out a sales invoice the computer posts it to the relevant accounts and at the end of each month and tax period you can run off the totals to give you the figures needed for your VAT return. And the same with purchases.

There are several packages around, so before you buy one make sure you know what you want to record. If you run a shop you will want stock control, whereas if you run a service business you will want debtor information. With a computer you can see at a glance the situation at a given time.

The important thing to remember with computers is that they only do what they are told. You will still need to make sure you have got your tax points right and that you have posted the right invoices to the right tax periods. You also have to make sure the liability is right and that your input tax can be reclaimed. It is no use blaming the computer for mistakes you make.

Computers and the VAT Office

Once you start using a computer you have to let the local VAT office know as soon as possible. They may send someone out to have a look at your machine or they may do nothing. Either way you can rest easy, knowing that if your particular package has a flaw concerning VAT they will tell you about it.

If at the end of the day you decide you can manage perfectly well with a simple set of books, then stay with them, for at least you can see what is happening at a glance.

Correcting Errors and the VAT Account

Because of default interest and serious misdeclaration penalty (see Chapter 1) there is a special way of correcting errors you discover yourself in your VAT returns. If you find you have made a mistake, for example if you missed out a sales invoice, added up the VAT column wrongly or your accountant found an error when doing the annual audit, there are two ways of correcting that mistake, depending on how much VAT is involved. This only applies to errors, so normal practice like reclaiming input in a later period, adjusting for credit notes, bad debt relief and retail schemes or partial exemption annual adjustments are not affected.

Error(s) of £1000 VAT or Less

The procedure here is to adjust for the error in your VAT account. It is a legal requirement to keep a VAT account which is simply a summary of totals taken from your various books and records which make up your VAT return. You have to detail the error as much as possible, so 'mistake from previous quarter' will not do.

Here is an example of a VAT account with an adjustment:

Period 03/96 VAT Account

Purchase Totals (from PDB	Net	VAT	Sales Totals (from SDB)	Net	VAT
January	100	17.50	January	200	35
February	100	17.50	February	200	35
March	100	17.50	March	200	35
	300	52.50		600	105
			Sales invoice 100 dated 1/1/94 missed from period 03/94	200	35
				800	140

If the adjustment is not in the VAT account it is treated as if the officer had discovered it and the interest *and* penalty, possibly, will apply.

Errors of More Than £1000 VAT

If the mistake(s) you discover amounts to more than £1000 owing either to you or to Customs and Excise, you have to write to your local VAT office telling them the amount of the mistake(s) and in which period it (or they) belongs. They send you an assessment for that amount with the interest but *not* the penalty. This is known as a voluntary disclosure.

8

Problem Areas

Cars · Change of Circumstance · Visits from the VAT Office

Cars

These have already been touched on, but they are something of a minefield as far as VAT is concerned. If, at this stage, you are debating buying a van instead of a car, then buy the van. You can reclaim the VAT on the purchase and on the running expenses with no other worries. But because cars are assumed to be for both business and pleasure there are all sorts of rules to ensure that you gain no advantage from being VAT registered. Customs and Excise define a car as being a passenger vehicle with all round windows and more than 1 but less than 12 seats.

Buying and Hiring

If you buy a car you cannot reclaim the VAT on the purchase. The only people who can are car dealers, and everyone else has to pay up. If you decide to hire or lease a car then you can reclaim the VAT but only as long as the ownership of the car never passes to you. This is because technically the hire or lease of a car is a supply of services and not the supply of a car. So do make sure you examine the small print of the contract to find out whether you are getting the car itself or merely the use of a car. Hire-purchase and lease-purchase agreements give you the car or the option to buy it, so the VAT cannot be reclaimed.

Input Tax on Running Expenses

If you do buy a car and use it in your business you can reclaim the VAT on repairs and maintenance. However, the input tax on the petrol or diesel you put in it is a much more complex affair. There are three ways of dealing with road fuel for cars in your business:

1 You reclaim *all* the input tax on *all* the petrol or diesel used in your car, whether for business *or* for private use. However, you have to pay back a set charge, called a scale charge, with every VAT return. This is to compensate for the fact that you are reclaiming the VAT on fuel used for private motoring. So even if you drive right round the coast of Britain every weekend for pleasure you can still reclaim the VAT on the fuel.

The charge you pay to Customs and Excise depends on the engine size of your car:

Frequency of VAT return	**Up to 1400cc**	**1401–2000cc**	**Over 2000cc**
1 Quarterly	£17.87 (£120)	£22.34 (£150)	£33.51 (£225)
2 Monthly	£5.96 (£40)	£7.45 (£50)	£11.17 (£75)
As 1 above but if you do over 4500 business miles per quarter	£8.94 (£60)	£11.17 (£75)	£16.83 (£113)
As 2 above but if you do over 1500 business miles per month	£2.98 (£20)	£3.72 (£25)	£5.66 (£38)

The amount in brackets is the actual scale charge which goes in your output box (box 4 on your VAT return) but this is not the amount which you pay. The output tax which is due to Customs and Excise is 7/47ths of the scale charge itself. If you use the reduced charge for big business mileage you have to be able to produce evidence to show that you did indeed travel more than the set number of miles.

2 You can decide to reclaim only the VAT on business mileage. But, as with the reduced scale charge, you have to keep detailed journey records to show that the VAT you are reclaiming relates only to fuel used on business trips.

3 You can choose *not* to reclaim any input tax for your car(s) and

not to pay any scale charges. But if you decide to do this you cannot reclaim VAT on road fuel for any other vehicle used in your business. So even if you run a road haulage firm, if you choose this option you cannot reclaim the VAT on even the lorries' road fuel. This is in fact Customs and Excise being generous to businesses where business mileage is very low and paying the scale charge would be uneconomical. It is an extra-statutory concession by Customs and Excise, which means they are under no obligation to operate it, but choose to do so.

If you take up this option you have write to your local VAT office to let them know.

Change of Circumstances

If any of your business details change you have to tell your local VAT office in writing within 30 days. It is very important that you remember to do so because you might be adversely affected if you do not. For example, if you change address and forget to tell Customs and Excise, your VAT returns will still be sent to your old one. If you then put them in late or not at all because of this you will end up with central assessments and surcharges (see Chapter 9). Here is a list of changes you should tell Customs and Excise about:

- Change of your principal place of business
- Change of your name or trading name
- Change of partners (as long as one partner stays the same) or their addresses
- Change of bank account details. Very important if you are a repayment trader or are on the annual accounting scheme
- Change in business activity, or trade class
- Change from limited company to unlimited company or vice versa

These changes only require a letter from you and will not affect your registration. More major changes to your business mean de-registration. These are:

- Closure or sale of your business
- Change of legal entity. If you change from a sole proprietor to a partnership or limited company or vice versa you have to fill in Form VAT 1 again, but you can ask to keep your VAT registration number
- Death, bankruptcy or liquidation. In these cases whoever takes on the business has to write in to the local VAT office

Visits from the VAT Office

From time to time Customs and Excise will remind you that they are more than just an address to write to or talk to by sending out one of their officers to have a look at your books and records. People have all sorts of ideas about Customs and Excise and their rumoured powers. Although the officer who visits you does have certain powers these are not as comprehensive as some people would like you to think.

Powers of Customs and Excise

- They can enter your premises at any *reasonable* time. So no night-time calls
- They can inspect your premises. This is *not* the same as a search which can only be done with a proper search warrant
- They can look at your books and records and take information from them
- They can take your books and records back to the VAT office. If they do this they have to give you access to them or copies so you can keep going
- They can take copies of your books and records
- They can demand books and records from another person (for example your accountant)
- They can demand that you produce books and records at your principal place of business. Ignore this one and you will get a £5 fine each day you delay
- They can demand information from you. You do not have to open your mouth to talk to a VAT officer but you might have to answer questions in writing
- They can demand to see your annual accounts
- They can take samples. This might be used where there is a liability problem
- They can make you open up a gaming machine
- They can inspect and check your computer(s) and any accessories
- They can issue an assessment to correct any mistakes

Before the Visit

18 to 30 months after registration you will get a telephone call from a VAT officer asking you for an appointment. If this proves difficult you will get a letter instead. If this causes you to worry it might be a

good idea to have another look through your books and records just to make sure you cannot spot any mistakes you might have made. If you do find any you can correct them by a voluntary disclosure or by adjusting your next VAT account (see Chapter 7). Do not be overawed by the visit but rather use it as an opportunity to ask questions. If you have any grey areas you want clearing up then ask for a decision in writing from the officer.

The Visit Itself

The first thing to remember is that a VAT officer is a human being like everyone else, so he or she is probably more worried about getting a cup of tea than about following your accounting system. If by some chance you find yourself with a less than friendly VAT officer then you should consider either not saying anything and/or writing in to complain. If you exercise your right to silence you may have to answer questions put in writing.

Usually just one person will turn up, but if two arrive then it is probably a training exercise or something internal, so there is no need to worry.

He or she will first want to have a chat with you about the business with perhaps a guided tour of the premises thrown in for good measure. If you have asked for the visit to take place at your accountant's the officer will still probably want to come and see you at your principal place of business.

The next step is for the officer to have a look through your books, records and any other bits and pieces you use in the running of your business, for example estimates, job cards and so on. If you stay close by then the officer can ask you as and if anything crops up which he or she does not understand. If your system is a difficult one to follow the officer might need you on hand to produce invoices or to indicate the audit trail.

Finally the moment of truth arrives and the officer tells you if any errors have been found in what has been examined. If there are any errors then you should get a detailed explanation of what has been done wrong. Always ask for a letter with any assessment in case you want to appeal (see the next chapter). If there are no mistakes reported it does not mean that there are none there, merely that the officer found none in the books and records he or she examined. So in theory another officer could come out the next day and look at a different area, find a mistake and issue an assessment.

Duration of the Visit

The length of each visit depends on how big and complex your business, books and records are. A small corner shop might only take a few hours whereas a multi-national might well last for months. It is worth remembering that VAT officers do not do anything like a full audit. As a VAT registered person it is your responsibility to account for VAT correctly, and the point of the VAT visit is to make sure you are doing just that, no more, no less.

The Next Visit

Again this will depend on the size and complexity of your business and accounting system. It also depends on what sort of trader you are. The ones who get it wrong all the time get visits all the time. If you are a model business then you should only get an occasional visit. Note that repayment traders get visited in the same way as payment traders, as after all there is still scope for mistakes to be made.

The Assessment

This can involve either demanding money from you or giving you some back. If you receive an assessment telling you that you owe Customs and Excise there are two courses of action open to you. You can either pay up and forget about it, or appeal because you do not agree with the VAT officer's ruling. What to do if you decide to appeal is the subject of the next chapter, Chapter 9: When Things Go Wrong.

9

When Things Go Wrong

Mistakes Found on VAT Visits · Late VAT Returns and Payment · VAT Tribunals

Mistakes Found on VAT Visits

If a VAT officer finds a mistake during a VAT visit he or she will send you an assessment to correct it. Naturally, if it is money due to you the chances are that you will not want to appeal against it. However, if the assessment demands money from you then you will certainly want to make sure that there is no mistake being made.

Remember that VAT officers are not infallible and they may issue assessments which are based on a wrong interpretation of the law. Of course as the trader you are at a disadvantage because a VAT officer spends his or her working life immersed in VAT and its complexities. If you are to get an assessment after a visit make sure you know exactly what it is for. You should be sent a letter setting out the facts and figures. Generally speaking, there are two types of mistake:

1 Accounting Errors

This is where you make a book-keeping slip. Perhaps you added a column of figures wrongly or you did a calculation with the wrong set of figures. The chances are that with this sort of mistake you should be able to see at a glance what you did or did not do. If you agree with the VAT officer then you will have to pay up without going any further.

2 Judgment Errors
These include things like liability or determining the status of input tax, for example whether it relates to an exempt supply or a taxable supply. This area is always a very thorny one and it is generally best to appeal in such a case. Land and property especially involve liability of nightmarish proportions. If you are not 100% clear about the supply you are making, the chances are that the VAT officer is not either. The problem arises here too of the VAT leaflets. These are Customs and Excise's *interpretation* of the law, not the law itself. If you go and see a specialist accountant or lawyer they may well be able to advise you of how the law relates to your situation.

The Local Appeal

Having received your assessment you might well want to discuss the matter with your accountant before going any further. He or she should have a good idea about whether or not an appeal would be successful, and would probably be willing to do all the work on your behalf if you cannot face it yourself.

Appealing locally means writing to your local VAT office to ask formally for a local reconsideration. You can also use this procedure to ask for a local reconsideration of other decisions made by Customs and Excise (for example if they send you a penalty for late registration).

All it will cost you is the time to write the letter and the postage stamp to get it there. You can go straight to a tribunal if you want to but it is much better to go through the local procedure first. In your letter you should quote your VAT registration number, the date and amount of the assessment together with your reasons for dispute. You have to do this within 30 days of the date of the assessment so do not spend too much time making your mind up.

The Local Decision

Once your letter asking for a reconsideration is received the issue at question is examined, usually by someone other than the officer who originally came out to see you. Once this has been done you will get a letter which will do one of two things:

1 Support the Original Assessment and/or Decision
If this happens and you are still convinced that you are in the right, you then have 21 days from the date of this letter to appeal to a VAT tribunal (more on this later). If you decide not to go any further you will have to pay up.

2 Change the Original Assessment and/or Decision
If you still disagree, for example if the assessment is reduced instead of being withdrawn, you can still appeal to a VAT tribunal. You have to appeal within 30 days of the letter telling you of the change.

Late VAT Returns and Late Payment

Your VAT return and any money due have to be with Customs and Excise by the date shown on your return form (the VAT 100). If you send a post-dated cheque dated after the 'due date' this still counts as a late payment. If your return and payment are submitted late then you are in default. The only people this does not affect are repayment traders, as Customs and Excise are not going to worry if you do not claim any money due to you.

The Default Surcharge

This is what you get if you persistently put in late returns and payments. If you put in two late returns and payments in any period of 12 months then you are sent what is called a Surcharge Liability Notice (SLN). This will tell you that if you do not get your act together and get your next 12 month's VAT returns and payments in on time you will be surcharged. This works in stages, so if you are in default again in the next 12 months you get first a 5% surcharge, then 10%, 15%, 20%, 25% up to a top limit of 30% of the tax you are due.

Central Assessments

If you do not put in your VAT return at all you will receive a central assessment. Customs and Excise make a guess at what you should be paying and send you a bill. If you continue not putting in returns these central assessments will keep on going up in value *and* there will be surcharges as well (see above). The surcharge stays, even if you do get round to putting your returns in eventually. All that happens is that Customs and Excise recalculate the percentage as a proportion of the figure you declare on the return itself.

It is worth noting that there is no appeal against a central assessment. If you continually pay on assessment instead of putting returns in, the chances are that you will be visited pretty promptly to see what is really going on. If the central assessments are then found to be too low you will get another assessment (which you cannot appeal against) to bring you up to what you should have paid. And there will be default interest and possibly the serious misdeclaration penalty as well.

So the golden rule is, always put your VAT return and money in on time, every time. If you can foresee any problems, for example you might have to go into hospital, then get in touch with your local VAT office for their advice. Once you get a surcharge you have to go through the appeals procedure to try to get rid of it again.

VAT Tribunals

These are independent bodies who referee your dispute with Customs and Excise when your local appeal is refused. You can go straight to a tribunal with your arguments but you are much better off going through the local reconsideration procedure first. You can ask for a local appeal against any decision Customs and Excise make about you, for example if they refuse to let you use the cash accounting or a retail scheme. If you are considering going to a tribunal the publication you will need is 'Appeals and applications to the tribunals'. It is in fact issued by the president of the VAT tribunals but you can get a copy from your local VAT office.

Time Limits

If, after a local reconsideration, Customs and Excise uphold their original decision, you have 21 days from the date you are informed to appeal to a VAT tribunal. If they change their minds you have 30 days from the date of the letter to appeal. It is very important that you stay within these time limits. Appeal too late and you may get nowhere. If that happens you have to write to the tribunal for an extension together with your excuse for being late.

What Can be Appealed Against

Here is a list of what you can dispute at a tribunal. Note that it does not include misdirection by a VAT officer. As mentioned in Chapter 1, if you have a case here your only appeal is by judicial review or by suing the Commissioners of Customs and Excise for negligence.

- You can dispute an assessment itself or how much it is for.
- You can dispute your registration or its cancellation.
- You can dispute not being allowed group registration or changing your present one.
- You can dispute penalties, surcharges, interest and how much

they are for. You can present your case here on grounds of 'reasonable excuse' but it has to be a good one. Serious unforeseen illness is your best bet. The only excuses *not* accepted are having no money and reliance on someone else.

- You can dispute not being allowed voluntary registration or exemption from registration.
- You can dispute the liability of supplies.
- You can dispute VAT charged on imports whether for yourself or for someone else's private goods.
- You can dispute what input tax you can reclaim.
- You can dispute bad debt relief claims.
- You can dispute do-it-yourself house claims.
- You can dispute not being allowed to use a retail scheme, cash or annual accounting.
- You can dispute having to give security for VAT due.
- You can dispute directions about the value of your supplies.
- You can dispute directions about computer invoices.
- You can dispute directions requiring different people to be registered as one person.

Before the Appeal

A tribunal will only hear your case if you have put in all your VAT returns and paid all VAT due, including any assessments. This does not apply to surcharges, penalties or interest. The only way to get out of this is to prove hardship to Customs and Excise or to the tribunal. Tribunals do not charge for their services but you and Customs and Excise can ask for costs. Customs and Excise normally only ask for costs where they consider you to be wasting their time, for example if you do not turn up or the matter is so clear as to not need a tribunal decision.

At and After the Appeal

Tribunals are fairly informal. You can represent yourself or get your accountant or solicitor along instead. If you do decide to do it yourself make sure you are properly organised, with your wits sharpened for the verbal cut and thrust with the representative from Customs and Excise. One of the problems you will have is that you have to prove that you are right, rather than Customs and Excise having to prove that you are wrong (unless it is a tax evasion case).

If you have lost you can appeal to a higher court but this is where things start to get very expensive. If you win you can ask for your money back, with interest.

Conclusion

The best way to avoid all these problems is by:

- Putting all your returns in on time with the right payment and,
- Making sure you are declaring the right tax at the right time and,
- Keeping up with all developments and pestering your local VAT office in writing if you are even slightly unsure of anything.

If you do all of these and still encounter problems because of the bureaucracy then write to your Member of Parliament. I did that once to the Inland Revenue. I was trying to get some tax back where I had earned under the tax allowance for the year. A year of letters got nowhere but a letter to my MP produced the money in a week. Dealing with the civil service can be like banging your head against a brick wall. At least if it is happening to you it is happening to others too.

Best of luck in your dealings with Customs and Excise.

Glossary

Agent Someone who does business on behalf of someone else (the principal), where the supply is from the principal to the final customer.
Annual accounting A scheme designed for the VAT weary trader who can meet certain conditions, it involves 9 monthly payments by direct debit in the year, with the 10th made by filling in the annual VAT return.
Annual adjustment If you have exempt input tax or use certain of the retail schemes you have to look at the whole year's activity at the end of each tax year (the VAT return ending March, April or May), by doing a calculation for the year.
Apportionment The process of splitting a single figure to find, for example, the proportion zero-rated and standard-rated of a supply.
Assessment A bill from Customs and Excise. A local one corrects errors found in your books whereas a central assessment is issued if you fail to put in your VAT return. It will also increase in value if you continue to miss your returns.
Bad debt relief The only way you can get back the VAT you had to pay on a bad debt is by writing it off in your accounts 1 year after the original supply was made.
Capital goods scheme This scheme operates if you buy a computer costing more than £50,000 and/or land and buildings costing more than £250,000. You have to adjust the input tax over a set number of years according to the changing taxable/exempt supplies they are used for.
Cash accounting A scheme whereby you can account for output tax on the basis of payment rather than invoice. There are certain conditions attached.

Change of Legal Entity (COLE) This is what you have to apply for if your entity or status changes, for example from a partnership to a limited company. It involves filling in form VAT 1 again.
Clawback If you reclaim input tax for a taxable supply and then change the supply to an exempt one, you have to repay the input tax you reclaimed to Customs and Excise. And vice versa.
Consideration Whatever you receive when you sell something, not necessarily money. VAT is always due on the open market value, as if you had only received money.
Daily gross take The total amount that you sell in a given day.
De minimis The limits set by Customs and Excise to determine if you are fully taxable or partially exempt. They have to be applied at the end of each tax year as well as each quarter you make exempt supplies.
Default interest Interest charged on errors either discovered by Customs and Excise, or, on voluntary disclosures.
Deferred accounting A system of paying VAT due on imports in the middle of the month after the import took place by direct debit.
Default surcharge An extra sum to pay if you keep sending in returns late or not at all. It goes up with every return put in late up to a maximum of 30%.
Directly attributable input tax Input tax which can be related specifically to either taxable or exempt supplies.
Disbursement Something you arrange on behalf of your customer but where the supply by-passes you. Examples include stamp duty, road tax or rates.
Exempt Not taxable, i.e. exempt from VAT.
Exempt input tax All the input tax which relates to exempt supplies.
Extra statutory concession Sometimes Customs and Excise allow these, even though in law they do not have to.
Fully taxable If you are fully taxable you are below the de minimis limits regarding your exempt input tax. You can therefore claim it all back.
Inputs Your purchases and business expenses, including imports.
Input tax VAT you are charged, mostly deductible on business expenses and purchases, sometimes not.
Intending trader Registration before you are up and running.
Less detailed tax invoice An invoice for less than £50 which only need show modified details.
Liability The liability of a supply is whether a supply is standard-rated, zero-rated, exempt or outside the scope of VAT.

Local VAT office (LVO) The place that looks after your VAT affairs.
Mark-up Profit divided by cost. Customs and Excise always talk of mark-ups rather than margins.
Non-attributable input tax Input tax which relates to both taxable and exempt supplies, and which has to be apportioned.
Non-standard tax periods Tax periods which are neither monthly nor quarterly but run from and to specific dates.
Notification The act of telling your local VAT office that you have to register. It involves filling in form VAT 1.
Option to tax If you rent or lease out commercial property you can, if you wish, change the liability from exempt to standard-rated. This means any related input tax can be reclaimed but once made, the decision is irrevocable.
Outputs Your sales (taxable and exempt) and your other business income.
Output tax VAT you charge your customers on behalf of Customs and Excise.
Outside the scope A supply is outside the scope if it is neither taxable nor exempt, for example a supply made not in the course of business.
Partial exemption You are partially exempt if your exempt input tax goes over the de minimis limits.
Postponed accounting For certain postal imports you use this system of accounting for the VAT. You charge yourself the output tax and reclaim it as input tax (subject to your partial exemption position, etc.).
Principal The person on whose behalf an agent acts.
Principal place of business (PPOB) The address where you are registered and the centre of your business activity.
Pro forma invoice This is merely advice of a supply and not a proper tax invoice. It cannot be used to reclaim input tax.
Repayment trader This is what you are if you always reclaim VAT on your returns.
Retail export If you are a retailer you can operate the retail export scheme, whereby your overseas customers can have the VAT they paid refunded.
Retail scheme A special calculation, only for retailers, to enable output tax to be worked out.
Reverse charge This is the output tax you have to charge yourself if you receive certain supplies from overseas.
Scale charge A set amount you have to pay to Customs and Excise

to account for the input tax on private road fuel you are reclaiming.

Second-hand scheme Certain goods qualify for this scheme, which involves only accounting for output tax on the difference between the buying and the selling price (the margin).

Self-billing A system where the customer issues the 1 invoice for a supply. This one invoice is the supplier's sales invoice and the purchaser's purchase invoice.

Self-supply A supply from you to you. The 2 main examples are in the construction industry and if you produce your own stationery. Output tax has to be accounted for. Reclaiming it depends on your partial exemption position.

Serious misdeclaration penalty (SMP) Mistakes found by Customs and Excise can get this penalty if they are 30% or more of the VAT actually due, or, if they are £10,000 and 5% or more of the VAT actually due. The penalty is 20% of the mistake.

Special method Any way you can think of which splits your non-attributable input tax into exempt and taxable input tax. This method needs approval.

Standard method A method, based on inputs, of splitting your non-attributable input tax into exempt and taxable input tax. This method does not need approval.

Standard-rated 17.5% VAT charged on everything not specifically zero-rated or exempt.

Tax invoice A document which records a supply and creates a tax point. It is the evidence needed to reclaim input tax.

Tax period The length of time, usually 3 months, covered by the tax return.

Tax point The date when output tax has to be accounted for.

Taxable person The entity which is, or should be, registered for VAT.

Taxable supply A supply which is taxed, either at the standard rate or at the zero rate.

Transfer of a going concern (TOGC) Where a business is taken over and certain conditions can be met. The VAT registration number can also be transferred, though this is not generally advisable as any debts get transferred as well.

Trade class (T/C) The number allocated to a particular business activity.

VAT 1 The registration form. Partnerships also have to fill in form VAT 2 which asks for details of the partners.

VAT 100 The return form.

VAT fraction To get the VAT element from the final selling price, you multiply by the VAT fraction

$$\frac{\text{Rate of Tax}}{100 + \text{Rate of Tax}} = \frac{17\tfrac{1}{2}}{117\tfrac{1}{2}} = \frac{7}{47}$$

VAT registered person The term given to the entity in business. It can be a sole proprietor, partnership, limited company, club, charity or association. The registration covers all the business activities of that VAT registered person.

VAT return The form where you tell Customs and Excise how much VAT you have charged and have been charged over the tax period.

VAT tribunal If you do not agree with a decision of Customs and Excise you can appeal to an independent VAT tribunal.

VAT central unit (VCU) Where your returns go to for processing.

Zero-rated A zero-rated supply is still a taxable supply, but the rate of tax has been set at zero.

Index